Strength & Courage for Caregivers

30 Hope-Filled Morning and Evening Reflections

ALSO BY TERRY D. HARGRAVE

Loving Your Parents When They Can No Longer Love You

Strength & Courage for Caregivers

30 Hope-Filled Morning and Evening Reflections

Terry Hargrave

ZONDERVAN.com

ZONDERVAN.com/
AUTHORTRACKER
follow your favorite authors

We want to hear from you. Please send your comments about this book to us in care of zreview@zondervan.com. Thank you.

ZONDERVAN®

Strength and Courage for Caregivers
Copyright © 2008 by Terry Hargrave

Requests for information should be addressed to:
Zondervan, *Grand Rapids, Michigan 49530*

Library of Congress Cataloging-in-Publication Data

Hargrave, Terry D.
 Strength and courage for caregivers : 30 hope-filled morning and evening
reflections / Terry D. Hargrave.
  p. cm.
 ISBN-10: 0-310-27769-8 (hardcover : alk. paper)
 ISBN-13: 978-0-310-27769-9 (hardcover : alk. paper)
 1. Caregivers--Prayers and devotions. I. Title.
BV4910.9.H37 2007
242'.4--dc22

                  2007045566

This edition printed on acid-free paper.

Interior design by Christine Orejuela-Winkelman

Printed in the United States of America

08 09 10 11 12 13 14 15 • 26 25 24 23 22 21 20 19 18 17 16 15 14 13 12 11 10 9 8 7 6 5 4 3 2 1

Contents

Foreword

I don't know which is worse—having a terminal disease or watching those you love have a terminal disease. I have a terminal disease. It is called amyotrophic lateral sclerosis (ALS), or Lou Gehrig's disease. ALS is a degenerative, incurable, and terminal disease. The average life span for people with ALS is two to five years. I am fortunate. I have had the disease for seven years and have a rare, slow-growing form of the disease. As I've watched my wife, children, and grandchildren deal with this disease, I am convinced that it is more difficult to watch someone you love deal with a terminal disease than to actually deal with the disease yourself.

Being a caregiver is not easy—and it is a never-ending task. You are called on to be there 24/7. Recently, I wrote a book of prayers and promises for those who are terminally ill. It is a book out of my own journey in dealing with this disease. It speaks to the fears and struggles of those who know they are going to die. And it offers hope in the midst of the darkness. I am so grateful that Terry Hargrave has written a book for caregivers. Caregivers tend to get overlooked when facing a serious illness. You will find his book to be honest, funny, and thought-provoking. Most of all, you will find it to be encouraging.

Every caregiver ought to read this book. Whether you are the primary caregiver or part of a larger circle of people who help, this is the book for you. I would also recommend that the persons being cared for read this book as well. It will give them insights into the struggles and challenges faced by those who help them every day. Dealing with a terminal disease is no easy task. And being a caregiver—especially the primary caregiver—is no easy task either.

One of the challenges of being a caregiver is that you really don't have much time for yourself. The morning prayers and evening reflections in this book are short and to the point. This is especially good for those who are ill and for those who care for them.

Ed Dobson, author of *Prayers and Promises When Facing a Life-Threatening Illness*

Introduction

There are some forty million of us out there currently, and we are a growing group. We are the group that provides some type of care to a family member, friend, neighbor, or loved one. As caregivers, we have a special place in God's heart as we learn the practice of attending to others' needs in a loving and unselfish manner. In my opinion, few things in life shape us as people and make the fruit of the Spirit come to life more than the consistency of caregiving. But it is not an easy job. As caregivers, we need support, respite, and daily encouragement.

The purpose of *Strength and Courage for Caregivers* is to give you some of that support, respite, and encouragement. Each day for thirty days, you will read a Morning Prayer and an Evening Reflection, which are intended to help you as a caregiver do what I consider to be the most essential elements in the caregiving job, namely, to embrace and accept the job as caregiver, learn the lessons about how to give care, and aspire to the character of Christ. Although each reflection relates to one of these three elements, they are interspersed throughout the book to give a balanced reading.

As you will read in these pages, my knowledge of caregiving comes from directing a personal care home and caring for my mother-in-law, Genevieve, with my wife, Sharon. Caregiving taught me who I was and how I could become a more godly man. As you read each morning and evening reflection, I hope and pray that they will direct you to a more fulfilling relationship with God, a more profound sense of the important role you fulfill, and an awareness of how God regards you, a caregiver, as utterly special and wonderful.

DAY 1

Morning Prayer

May I See the Hidden Purposes of God

Consider it pure joy, my brothers, whenever you face trials of many kinds, because you know that the testing of your faith develops perseverance. Perseverance must finish its work so that you may be mature and complete, not lacking anything.

JAMES 1:2–4

Every caregiver, no matter how patient, loving, and caring, eventually comes to the end of his or her rope. At those times, you want to grab hold of the one you care for and bark, "Just do as I say!" With your other hand, you want to shake a fist at God and shout, "Why are you doing this to me?"

For me, one of these days came when I received a call from the retirement facility where my mother-in-law, Genevieve, lived. "We think she's had a stroke," they reported.

I went to Genevieve's apartment and found her disoriented, with slurred speech and one side of her body partially paralyzed. I took her to the emergency room because I too was convinced she had had a stroke. When the neurologist was called in, she also suspected we would find brain damage, as she ordered blood tests and an MRI. My wife, Sharon, and I comforted her mother as we calmly talked about what this new level of caregiving would mean for our family and our lives.

Then the neurologist came back to the room with a sheepish grin on her face. She pointed to the sheet containing the lab results and said, "We were wrong. She didn't have a stroke; she's drunk."

As her words sank in, I began to realize that all of my patient and loving concern for my mother-in-law had been a waste. She had somehow fallen back into the alcoholism that had dogged her for most of her adult life. "How did she get ahold of alcohol?" I wondered. Doesn't she know how dangerous it is for someone in her fragile condition to drink? Doesn't she know that drinking will complicate her suspected Alzheimer's disease? Doesn't she realize the sacrifices I've made to care for her? Doesn't she appreciate anything I've done? Doesn't she realize how much her drinking insults me?

All of these questions ran through my mind, and there I was—grabbing her with one hand and shaking my fist at God with the other. I yelled at her. I cursed at her. I did my best to humiliate her.

As I helped Genevieve into the car to take her back home, I began to reflect on my actions. Here was a woman who bravely raised her four young children after her husband died. She had suffered through the untimely deaths of her two older children, yet continued to work and hold a home together. She was willing to sacrifice all she had for the good of her two remaining kids and her grandchildren. Yet all I could see was a person—whom I was trying to care for—not cooperating and greatly complicating my life.

I was mad at Genevieve for not making my acts of service and love to her easy, and I was mad at God for not making her obedient and cooperative. But as my yelling and cursing echoed through my head, I realized without a doubt that God had a very different purpose in mind from just our taking care of Genevieve. This was a loving and sacrificial woman with a drinking problem. I was an impatient, unloving, and uncaring man who was acting in judgmental and self-righteous ways. Just who was God trying to teach?

As I drove back home, I said a prayer and humbled myself before God. Instead of yelling at God, "Why are you doing this to me?" I was beginning to realize just why God was at work. He is at work in every caregiver's life to forge a godly character that will not only reflect Christ but also testify to his love and service and bring glory to his name.

Teach me, God. Teach me real patience, real love, and real care. Today, and every day, I want to be a person who clearly sees your hidden purpose in caregiving— to change and conform my life and character to reflect Christ.

Evening Reflection

Doing a Job Nobody Wants

> It is God who works in you to will and to act
> according to his good purpose.
>
> PHILIPPIANS 2:13

I am a counselor by trade. Although in my younger days the idea of being a counselor was much more glamorous, the reality is quite different. I feel great joy and satisfaction in helping people, yet sometimes the suffering of my clients overwhelms me. Most people who come to counselors are in deep life messes that are born out of depression, shame, trauma, selfishness, pride, infidelity, addictions, perversions, dishonesty, or just plain sinfulness. I often say, "The true problems people bring to counseling are much more difficult than any fiction they could invent." Sometimes I feel like an ER doctor, staring down at the mangled victim of a terrible accident. I hardly know which wound to treat first. And these life problems and the issues that caused them are not easily given up or changed. Most of counseling is slow, often painful, and very messy work.

Caregiving often brings us the physical messes that counseling delivers on the emotional side. Sometimes the people that need our care were put in that condition through no fault of their own. Perhaps the person was born with a special need or contracted an ailment. Maybe he suffered some accident or mishap. Maybe she behaved recklessly or failed to care for herself properly.

No matter how these persons came to be in our care, they now have problems they cannot take care of themselves. And we, their caregivers, see that caregiving will most likely be a slow, sometimes painful, and unusually messy work. It is not a job most people look forward to doing and probably one they avoid whenever possible.

It is always that way with work that is eternal and really important. Remember the story Jesus told about the Good Samaritan? A priest and a Levite both saw a man on the road badly in need of care. But somehow these men were able to reason with themselves that it was not their job to care for the stranger, or maybe that the business they were occupied in was just too important to allow them to get weighed down by the obvious need of a victim.

But the Samaritan was different:

He went to him and bandaged his wounds, pouring on oil and wine. Then he put the man on his own donkey, took him to an inn and took care of him. The next day he took out two silver coins and gave them to the innkeeper. "Look after him," he said, "and when I return, I will reimburse you for any extra expense you may have."

LUKE 10:34–35

Jesus smartly asks, "Who was the one who really loved?" Real love reaches out to the one in need. It reaches out not because it is easy, glamorous, or even full of recognition. In fact, the truest form of love is the sacrificial giving in which we are likely never to be paid back. True love involves just us, the person who needs us, and the love in our hearts. Caregiving is not an easy job, nor is it particularly desirable, but as James points out, pure religion and pure love involve caring for those who have nothing and cannot care for themselves (James 1:27).

Hardly anyone enters the job of caregiving without thinking at times, "*What* have I gotten myself into?" But take heart. God who loves us so supremely takes particular joy when we mimic his love in selfless ways. You did not pass by when you saw the need. Your heart was moved, and you took on the job of caregiving and all it entails. You do indeed understand the command to love your neighbor as yourself.

DAY 2

Morning Prayer

Now this is what the LORD Almighty says: "Give careful thought to your ways. You have planted much, but have harvested little. You eat, but never have enough. You drink, but never have your fill. You put on clothes, but are not warm. You earn wages, only to put them in a purse with holes in it." This is what the LORD Almighty says: "Give careful thought to your ways."

HAGGAI 1:5–7

I'm a guy who often gets priorities a bit mixed up. A few years ago, we were having a particularly difficult season of life. I was having some health problems, my wife and I were caring for her mother, both of our work schedules contained some challenging counseling clients, and we were both worn out.

So when my young daughter Halley Anne wanted to do something special for Valentine's Day dinner, I was a bit skeptical. I wanted to go out for dinner and have a pleasant evening as a family—with no cleanup at the end. What Halley Anne had in mind, however, was a five-course meal cooked at home and served on our finest china.

I knew what was in store. Sharon, my wife, would have to scour cookbooks to find the right recipes. While Halley Anne was a great cook, she was not a great cleaner, so I would have piles of dishes to wash. So in the end we compromised. We would have the dinner at home, but we'd cook only simple dishes.

Actually, things were going pretty well until the morning of February 14. That day, Sharon got up early to peel and shred potatoes for a particular casserole she and Halley Anne had picked out. Somehow, potato casserole did not fit my definition of "simple." "Why not just do baked potatoes?" I thought.

When I realized that all this was resulting in a more complicated preparation than I thought necessary, I went nuts! I yelled at Sharon for preparing a complicated dish. I yelled at Halley Anne for foisting such a complicated dinner on us. And I yelled at my son Peter for no particular reason. I gave everyone a piece of my mind I could ill afford to lose.

Then I walked into the dining room. Among the fine china were beautiful placemats with cupids and hearts. Brass napkin rings with hearts and arrows contained matching napkins. "Where did these come from?" I snapped.

Sharon answered, "Halley Anne used her own money to buy these. She wanted to make the dinner special."

Don't you just hate those moments of silence where just seconds before you were convinced you had a really good point but now realize you've been making a total jerk of yourself? I was in the throes of one of these moments. All my daughter wanted to do was to make Valentine's Day special, and she was willing to go to great lengths (and cost) in order to make it happen. Yet I had ruined her day because of potato casserole. If that isn't the consummate definition of "small potatoes," then I don't know what is. If only I would have embraced what my daughter was doing that day and made it more special. If only I would have looked to the importance of relationships instead of my own schedule.

We went on with the dinner (and made a decent recovery), but I have never forgotten the lesson. But the lesson was not about making a mountain out of a molehill—making small things bigger than they really are. Rather, I began to look for the small things in life that are really important.

At that time, I was so consumed with my health. But now I honestly can't tell you what was hurting or wrong. At that time, we were so stressed with the needs of clients. But I can't remember any of their names. All that seemed so important at the time was swept under the heavy rug of the passage of years. But Halley Anne's effort—a very small, thoughtful gesture—I will remember for a lifetime with a smile on my face. God often uses very small things to shape our characters and teach us big life lessons.

Today, many important, pressing items will demand our time and attention as caregivers., We won't remember most of them in the years to come—the name of that medication that seemed so important to ask the doctor about, the loads of laundry or even the particular clothes we washed, the stress we felt, except for some vague feeling of past difficulty.

This is what we will remember: our efforts to make small connections. We will recall words of endearment. We will remember the times we stroked their hair, the times they squeezed our hands and thanked us. These are the small things we will remember in the years to come.

May we learn to look to the small things in life that will make a big difference.

Evening Reflection

Called to Be a Caregiver

"Come, follow me," Jesus said, "and I will make you fishers of men."
At once they left their nets and followed him.

MATTHEW 4:19–20

One day, early in Jesus' ministry, he was strolling on the beach and saw Peter and Andrew plying their trade of fishing. He called to them, and immediately they left their nets and followed him. Why did they do such a crazy thing? Perhaps they sensed the tremendous power of Jesus, or perhaps they were fascinated with his reputation. But there was little doubt that they followed because Jesus issued a call on their lives. It was simple, straightforward, and immediate. Like their ancestor Abraham, they set out with Jesus, not knowing where they were heading or where they would end up. They simply followed.

The call to caregiving is not so simply stated. Most of us will not hear the voice of God or even feel a confirmed prompting calling us to give care. Instead, we'll clearly see there is a need. A child is born with a severe disability; a loved one is injured or becomes ill; an elderly person is deteriorating. Is the need sufficient for the call? I think so. If we are followers of Jesus, then we follow him to the places where he is called to serve.

We are called to love, to serve, and even to suffer. First John 3:17–19 reminds us: "If anyone has material possessions and sees his brother in need but has no pity on him, how can the love of God be in him? Dear children, let us not love with words or tongue but with actions and in truth. This then is how we know that we belong to the truth, and how we set our heart at rest in his presence." I don't interpret this to mean that we will always serve or give perfectly out of clean and unselfish hearts, but I do believe we have the call of Christ on our hearts to give ourselves to the needy. When a person is in need of care and we have the ability to care, then it is our job—our calling—to be the caregiver.

You have obviously responded to that call because you have seen the need. You realize that you may not always do the job right, but you are trying to respond with the love of God to a person who needs you. But naturally you worry that the job of caregiving will take you away from other responsibilities and that you may lose your career or livelihood. What's more, you don't know how much good the caregiving will actually do in the long run.

The truth is that none of us know what will happen. When we accept the job of caregiving, we are like the disciples or like Abraham when they received their call from God. We set out on a pathway, not knowing where the way leads or how we will be changed during the process of the journey. We just follow. Caregiving may indeed result in a blurring of family responsibilities. It may entail a change in career or end in the death of the one we care for or in our own death. So why would we do such a crazy thing?

We follow the call of caregiving because we believe that God's purposes in us will ultimately be achieved, and that we will be perfected to the likeness of the most loving and most caregiving Christ. The apostle Paul promises, "We know that in all things God works for the good of those who love him, who have been called according to his purpose. For those God foreknew he also predestined to be conformed to the likeness of his Son, that he might be the firstborn among many brothers" (Romans 8:28–29).

The call of caregiving is the call to be like Christ. Caregiving is sometimes confusing and usually physically and mentally exhausting. But the call has a specific purpose in our lives. The call ultimately works good in our lives by bringing us closer to God. That purpose is the promise we strive for and is at the heart of why we give care. Let us hold fast to the promise.

DAY 3

Morning Prayer

May I Be Courageous

*Do not be anxious about anything, but in everything, by prayer
and petition, with thanksgiving, present your requests to God.
And the peace of God, which transcends all understanding, will
guard your hearts and your minds in Christ Jesus.*

PHILIPPIANS 4:6–7

I have a saying my family makes fun of. I say it, really, when I
don't know what else to say. I said it the time my son was worried about how he did on a test, the time my wife was concerned
about how to help a counseling client, the time a friend was
concerned about whether he'd make it financially—and all those
times people asked me whether their physical, financial, and
emotional resources were adequate for the demands of caregiving. All these times I use this saying: "We just don't know what
is going to happen."

"Oh really," my family, friends, and clients say sarcastically.

I'm not trying to be a smart aleck, and I'm certainly not
trying to be trite. Actually, I'm trying to speak truth. I'm trying
to say there is no possible way for us to anticipate the future
enough to be able to control it. We can plan, prepare, and even
practice. But when the future arrives in the form of the present,
all we can do is take the available resources and forge ahead
with whatever God in his providence has handed to us.

When Jesus was in Gethsemane in the moments before he
was taken prisoner and then crucified, he cried out, "Father, if

you are willing, take this cup from me; yet not my will, but yours be done" (Luke 22:42). Make no mistake, Jesus was concerned about the future. The heartache, pain, and impending separation from God were overwhelming. It was as though Jesus was saying, "Man, I don't want to go through what's in store for me these next few days." But he also added, "But it is not up to me. It is up to you, God."

If Jesus could not control the future, then it is a given that we cannot either. All we can do is what Jesus did in his circumstance: he comforted himself with the knowledge that God would be with him. Did Jesus absolutely know that he would be up to the task? I don't think so. Not because I think Jesus was inadequate, but because if he thought he would have no trouble, he wouldn't have been so uneasy in the garden.

As caregivers, we really do face a world of uncertainty every day. Most weeks and almost every day, we face times when we simply don't know if our resources will be up to the challenge. We are in situations where we are extraordinarily unclear about what will happen next with the one we care for and whether his or her situation will worsen and our lives will be thrown into more turmoil. We dread the pain, the uncertainty, and the problems in the future. Be assured, "We just don't know what is going to happen."

We just don't know all the twists and turns of life. We just don't know how we will respond when stressed. We just don't know if we will be up to the task. But what we do know is powerful: we know the one who holds the future. We know that all that he does is somehow used in molding and making us into what he would have us be. We know that he loves us like no other. And we know that he will be there with us when the future comes. All we can do when we don't know what is going to happen is courageously hold on to him.

As a caregiver, may I be courageous enough to hold on to the living God. May I not focus on the pain or uncertainty but rather on the fact that God and I will work as colaborers in the situation that lies ahead. May I not be afraid to be fearful—only courageous enough to move forward and face what will happen next.

Evening Reflection

When Kindness Costs Something

Your attitude should be the same as that of Christ Jesus:

> *Who, being in very nature God,*
>   *did not consider equality with God*
>   *something to be grasped,*
> *but made himself nothing,*
>   *taking the very nature of a servant,*
>   *being made in human likeness.*
> *And being found in appearance as a man,*
>   *he humbled himself*
>   *and became obedient to death—*
>   *even death on a cross!*

PHILIPPIANS 2:5–8

Jackie Robinson, the first black player in major league baseball, suffered immeasurably during his first years playing for the Brooklyn Dodgers. Made to promise that he would not respond or retaliate in any way to the taunts, mistreatment, and physical abuse he received from players, fans, or teammates, Robinson forced down all the outrage and indignation at what he experienced and showed only stalwart kindness and patience. But he was abused. His legs and ankles were laced with wounds from players who spiked him with their shoes. He was spat at from the field, stands, and locker room. And he seldom went anywhere without hearing verbal grenades lobbed into his ears. He was black. He was different. He was alone.

On one occasion when the Dodgers were playing in another city, Robinson stepped out to wait for his turn at bat. As he took one knee, a flood of insults poured from the stands onto the field. Robinson did not turn around, nor did he respond. But on this particular occasion, his white teammate "Pee Wee" Reese, a Kentucky man well acquainted with bigotry and hatefulness toward blacks, stepped out of the dugout. Without saying a word, Reese took a knee beside Robinson. Then he slid his arm over the shoulder of Robinson.

Two teammates—one unwilling to let the other stand alone amid the insults and abuse. It was as though Reese was saying, "This is my pal. If you abuse him, you will have to abuse me right along with him." Make no mistake—Reese received much abuse as the result of his actions. His act of kindness and identification cost him something.

As caregivers, we do many things that can be considered loving, caring, and kind. We shop, cook, and clean. We bathe and help with hygiene. We feed and dress. We drive, we pay bills, we nurse, we seek medical care, we nurture—the list of things we do as caregivers is long and loving. But amidst all of those loving things that we do, none is more powerful than the kindness we show by identifying with the one who needs our care.

The fact is, we could pay another person to do all the tasks involved in caregiving. But we cannot pay for the tasks that say, "I love you, and you and I belong to each other."

In a very real sense, the person who needs us has been assaulted by life in some way. They have been taken down by disease, injury, or limitation. We could take care of them without ever connecting. But what a statement it makes when we slide out of our emotional dugout and take a knee beside the person who needs us. Symbolically, we put our arm over their shoulder and say, "We are in this thing together. Where we go and what we do, we learn, love, and live as teammates. You are my pal." This does cost us something, of course—our separate individuality and freedom.

Of course, this is what Jesus Christ did for us. It did cost Jesus also. His identification with us cost him ridicule and loss of his place, and eventually his life. But God exalted him for his sacrifice, kindness, and identification.

Of course we cannot save the whole world; we can't even save the one we care for. But when we identify with him or her, we give an accurate picture of what Christ Jesus did for us. God exalted Jesus for this sacrificial and kind act, and he will exalt us too for our caring work.

DAY 4

Morning Prayer

May I Remember "There Ain't No Small Thing"

> *Then the word of the LORD came to me: "The hands of Zerubbabel have laid the foundation of this temple; his hands will also complete it. Then you will know that the LORD Almighty has sent me to you. Who despises the day of small things? Men will rejoice when they see the plumb line in the hand of Zerubbabel."*
>
> ZECHARIAH 4:8–10

Sheryl, a lovely Southern woman, had a twenty-two-year-old son, Johnny, who "wasn't born quite right." He was unable to speak or walk, although there were times when he would make direct eye contact. Whether he understood anything that was going on around him was a question, but there was no question about Sheryl's commitment and love toward her son. She was fiercely loyal to him and absolutely devoted to making sure he got the proper care and nurture he needed. I would never see him looking ungroomed or in the least bit of distress.

But Sheryl was not a hovering mother. She had a full-time job as a cook in a diner, was involved in her church, and was the mother of two older children. Although she never told me directly, I suspected she never received any support from Johnny's father in terms of care, financial help, or concern. She was always positive and encouraging to everyone she met and was certainly one of the more capable caregivers I'd ever encountered.

"How do you get accomplished everything you do?" I asked her once.

"Honey," she said, "it's like building a strong wall. You lay in brick by brick until you get a life built. My neighbor looks in on Johnny when I'm at work; that's a brick. My sister comes by in the afternoon and gives Johnny lunch; that's another brick. Even Johnny—he can run a comb through his hair when I put it in his hand; that's another brick. You just keep laying in the bricks until you get that wall of your life built. One more thing I've learned: every brick is important. There ain't no small thing. Every brick in the building of life is important."

When the remnant of people returned to Jerusalem after years of captivity in Babylon, the prospect of rebuilding the wall, the city, their homes, and the temple looked too daunting. For years, even after the people had begun to scratch out their existence on their former land, the temple continued to lay in ruin. It was too big of a project, and they had to put all their effort into just making life work and getting food on the table. Besides, even if they were able to rebuild some semblance of a temple, it wouldn't even come close to the majestic beauty of Solomon's temple, which had been obliterated before the captivity. But with the encouragement of the prophets Haggai and Zechariah and the leadership of Zerubbabel, the people did indeed begin laying good brick on good brick, good stone on good stone.

"There ain't no small thing" when it comes to accomplishing God's work. The job of caregiving is complex, with a thousand details and things to do. At times it looks so daunting it appears impossible to accomplish. How do you do it? You pile one deed on another. You put in place one support system after another. You develop one routine after another. Before you know it, you've built the elements of a caregiving life that not only provides good care but also is doable. But you must get started piling the elements together. Each element is important in bringing together the practice of good care and your life as a caregiver. May we never forget that in caregiving, "there ain't no small thing."

Evening Reflection

My Mistakes and Failures

If we confess our sins, he is faithful and just and will forgive us our sins and purify us from all unrighteousness.

1 JOHN 1:9

One day I had to take my mother-in-law, Genevieve, to the doctor. So I helped her into the car, cranked the engine, and started to pull away. Just then, I remembered that I wanted to take her medications to the appointment. As I opened the car door, I thought, "I really should turn off the car and take the keys."

But I didn't. I comforted myself with the thought that I'd only be a minute, and so I left the car running as I ran to get the medications.

When I returned minutes later, there sat Genevieve very peacefully. But when I tried to get in, I discovered that she had hit the button to lock the car. At that time, her dementia was such that she simply looked at me with a blank expression as I pleaded with her to unlock the door. She just couldn't understand what I was saying and what I needed her to do. Not only did we miss the doctor's appointment; I had to call a locksmith to get my car door opened.

Once when I was speaking to a woman with early stage Alzheimer's, I suggested she might want to share with her daughter some of the meaningful things she had said to me. "I don't think I could," she said, "because my daughter would be angry at me for sharing important details of our family with a stranger." It made me sad because I knew that the woman's daughter longed for intimate connection and conversation with her mother before her mother's mind slipped away. Often when therapists get involved with intimate details of story, they get closer to the client than his or her own family members because they are able to get to the heart of the issues in a way family members can't. Sometimes clients sense they've gotten too close to us too soon and respond by backing off from their families. Such was the case here. "If only I had given her the chance to process her thoughts a bit more and helped her see how to express herself," I thought to myself. But now the woman had rejected the idea, and it wasn't likely she would reconsider it for quite some time.

What do these two stories have in common? They represent the kind of mistakes and failures I make during the job of caregiving. Most of my mistakes and failures fit into two broad categories: doing the wrong thing, such as making a wrong turn and getting stuck, and doing the right thing but doing it at the wrong time.

I have learned through my many years of caregiving that I will do the wrong things at the wrong times. I administer the wrong medication; I use poor judgment when moving a person in need; I drop him or her; I cook something that makes a person sick because it isn't good for his or her system; I say or do something insensitive that deeply hurts the feelings of the person for whom I give care.

There are other times when my actions are well reasoned and purposeful, but I end up pushing the right thing too hard or too quickly and it turns out to have a negative effect. How do I cope with my mistakes and failures? I do what most of us do. I hide my mistakes, defend them with my good intentions, or beat myself up with blame for not having made a different decision.

Caregiving isn't easy. Only after we have made the mistake do we see what we should have done or the timing that would have been better. As is commonly said, "The trick to making good decisions is experience. The way to get experience is through bad decisions."

The lesson I've learned through making many mistakes and experiencing many failures at caregiving is that my good intentions do not change outcomes. Mistakes and failures are what they are—and I must deal with the consequences. The promise that we have is that caregiving errors are no different from any other failure to do the right thing. We can still confess these errors and find forgiveness from the One who purifies us from unrighteousness.

This promise doesn't mean we won't have to clean up our messes, but it does mean we don't have to hide, and it certainly means we don't have to beat ourselves up for the errors. We all make mistakes; we all fail. Let us confess these issues, and then we can move on without condemnation.

DAY 5

Morning Prayer

May I Be Faithful One Day at a Time

> *"Well done, good and faithful servant! You have been faithful with a few things; I will put you in charge of many things. Come and share your master's happiness!"*
>
> MATTHEW 25:21

I walked into the personal care facility where I served as director to find chairs placed in the middle of the hall every twenty-five feet or so. The chairs led like a trail of bread crumbs to one of the wings of the facility where Dorothy's room was located. Although I was known to be an easygoing person in enforcing rules at our care facility, chairs in the middle of a walkway was a definite no-no for licensing and safety. When I anxiously asked one of the aides what was going on, she said, "Oh, you've got to see this one! Be patient and watch for Dorothy."

Dorothy was a ninety-six-year-old woman who had long been widowed. Within the last year she had suffered the grief of outliving her only daughter, who died of cancer. She had also fallen and broken her hip and had just returned from a four-month stay at a rehabilitation unit. From my perspective, Dorothy had every reason to throw in the towel and succumb to her grief and to physical deterioration. But she didn't.

Within a few minutes, Dorothy exited her room with her walker, slowly making her way down the hall. When she came to the first chair, she sat and rested for three or four minutes, then it was on to the next chair and another few minutes of rest. On and on Dorothy made her way down the hall until she reached her objective—the morning breakfast table.

I sat down beside Dorothy. "So," I congratulated her, "you found a way to make it to breakfast on your own."

She smiled. "You know, I can't do much, but I want to do all I can. I figured I may not be able to go for a walk, but I can walk enough to get to meals and get my mail. It may not be much, but it will keep me going."

Oh, to have the attitude of Dorothy! This frail old woman who could not do much had her heart set on doing what she could.

I may be much more "capable" than Dorothy. I may have more physical strength, mental acumen, more money, and more friends. But if I do not have the attitude she so richly possessed, I lose the optimism and pleasure of doing the work that God has set before me.

When Jesus taught about his second coming, he told a story about a master returning to the land he had put under the charge of a servant. Jesus reminded his listeners, "Who then is the faithful and wise servant, whom the master has put in charge of the servants in his household to give them their food at the proper time? It will be good for that servant whose master finds him doing so when he returns. I tell you the truth, he will put him in charge of all his possessions" (Matthew 24:45–47).

It wasn't easy for Dorothy to manage her life and do what she could. She had to be committed and then still find a way to make those four walks a day. But she faithfully performed whatever task she could as long as she had another day in front of her.

There are many challenges of patient servanthood ahead of me this day. There are issues I cannot solve. There are too many problems for my small capacity. But today, I want to be faithful to do what I can do. Although my efforts may be weak, frail, or incomplete, I want God to find me doing my best.

Evening Reflection

How to Be the Greatest

"Now that I, your Lord and Teacher, have washed your feet, you also should wash one another's feet. I have set you an example that you should do as I have done for you. I tell you the truth, no servant is greater than his master, nor is a messenger greater than the one who sent him. Now that you know these things, you will be blessed if you do them."

JOHN 13:14–17

He may have been the greatest boxer of all time. Muhammad Ali, with his quick feet and magician-like hands, would make boxing a spectacle as he outmatched opponent after opponent. His skills were equaled only by his loud and boisterous claim, "I am the greatest!"

Jesus' disciples wanted to be the greatest too. They were thrilled when Jesus performed unbelievable miracles and amazed at his glory in the transfiguration. Impressed, they started talking with each other about who among them would eventually become the greatest. At that point Jesus called a child over and said, "Whoever welcomes this little child in my name welcomes me; and whoever welcomes me welcomes the one who sent me. For he who is least among you all—he is the greatest" (Luke 9:48).

The disciples doubtless heard these words with their heads, but the words did not compute in their hearts. They were locked into a competition with each other and the rest of the world. They were interested in who would garner the most fame, the most riches, and the most glory. Sure, they were interested in doing good, but for the good they were doing they expected to be recognized and get just that much more fame and notoriety.

As caregivers, we aren't much different from the disciples. We long for appreciation and admiration. We may even want wealth, power, comfort, and security. In most cases, however, we put a good part of our lives on hold in order to give care. We rarely receive financial compensation for what we do, nor do we receive much recognition from family and friends for being good caregivers. Most of us, however, keep plugging away and giving the care. Have we learned to be the "least"? Certainly our actions appear to be loving. But sometimes we are motivated by ugly things, such as needing to alleviate guilt, wanting to keep up appearances, or even craving the sense that someone needs us.

We are only the "least" when we serve with selfless love and humility. We should never kid ourselves about how important true humility is. Jesus always saw the simple act of service given to the most needy as the true measure of greatness. He never used his care and compassion for the helpless to make a reputation for himself. How do we know this? First, Jesus strove to do things for people in secret. Over and over again he told those whom he had healed not to tell anyone. Second, we saw how Jesus behaved when he was not on the big stage of ministry. In perhaps one of the most humbling acts recorded in Scripture, Jesus took a basin of water and began to wash the feet of his disciples. He was not faking humility but instead humbly desired to serve and minister to those whom he loved the most.

Who is the greatest? Jesus. Who is the greatest among people? Those who humbly serve and care for others, just as Jesus humbly cared for others.

Muhammad Ali was indeed a great boxer. We remember him the way he was—dancing around the ring and making his outrageous rhymes—but Ali now has Parkinson's disease and is forced to receive help from humble caregivers. The greatest boxer of all time is cared for by people who are actually the greatest in God's economy.

Let us all as caregivers remember that we are given a great privilege each day as we keep our hearts pure and focused on God. We are not rich, powerful, or famous. But we are members of Jesus' elite club of those who serve and care for others. We are among a group that has the potential of being known as "the greatest."

DAY 6

Morning Prayer

May I Work for Reconciliation

Do not repay anyone evil for evil. Be careful to do what is right in the eyes of everybody. If it is possible, as far as it depends on you, live at peace with everyone.

ROMANS 12:17–18

It was one of the toughest caregiving situations I've ever seen, but, sadly, not unique. Noreen, a woman in her mid-fifties, had struggled to raise her three children. Her marriage, while committed, had severe communication and intimacy problems. And now here she was, caring for her oldest brother, an alcoholic who had suffered a stroke in his mid-sixties. Her other brother had long since renounced any responsibility for his older sibling, her parents were deceased, and her brother's drug-addicted son was in no shape to care for his father. This would have been a tough enough caregiving situation for anyone, but Noreen had a tremendous complicating factor: her oldest brother had sexually abused her when she was younger.

Every day Noreen struggled with her thoughts and feelings. "Why am I the one who has to care for him when he never cared for me?" she'd wonder. "How can I give care to someone who has doled out such injury to me? Am I sick for even thinking about doing the job?"

When Noreen and I talked about the possibility of her not being her brother's caregiver, she would come back to the fact that there was simply no one else to do the job. "I know," I said, "but that doesn't necessarily mean it is your job to do." But Noreen could not escape the conclusion that it was her duty to take care of her brother.

But Noreen did struggle. "Sometimes I just wish I could make him feel half of the hurt he caused me," she said.

"I understand," I told her. "You certainly are justified in feeling that way. But you know you can't hurt him and you won't hurt him. And since you won't give up the job of caring for him, you need *him* to address the hurt."

"He can speak only a few words and can barely move," she said. "How can he address my hurt?"

"I'm really not sure," I said. "But we are instructed in Romans 12:18 to be at peace with everyone, as far as it depends on us."

Noreen thought for a long time and said, "You are talking about forgiveness."

"Maybe," I said, "but currently you are doing a loving thing for your brother while hating him in your heart. I believe you must make what you *feel* and what you *do* match, or you will drive yourself crazy."

The next time I saw Noreen, her face showed she had reached a point of peace. When I asked what was different, she said, "I finally came to the conclusion that if I couldn't forgive him, I needed to stop being his caregiver. I decided to talk to him. I said, 'You know what you did to me as a little girl, and now I'm forced to clean, dress, and feed you. It isn't fair, and I've been trying to decide whether or not to forgive you or stop caring for you. I don't even know if you want to be forgiven.' At that point he gestured toward my hand and looked at me. Although he couldn't say it, he mouthed the word *please*. We stared at each other a long time, and I finally said, 'OK then, I will forgive you.' He looked at me and gave a long blink, which means *yes*. Everything certainly is not perfect, but at least my heart is now matching the care I'm giving him."

Some of us face having to give care to people who have caused us huge hurts and done us great wrongs for which they have never said they were sorry. But even if the hurt isn't as big as Noreen's, we all have a need to work toward reconciling. We do a good work, but our hearts need to be free of the pain of the past, where we do not wish evil while doing good caregiving. Today I want to seize the opportunity for reconciliation for both large and small hurts my charge has given me.

Evening Reflection

How Far Can Emotion Take Us?

"Each of you is to take up a stone on his shoulder, according to the number of the tribes of the Israelites, to serve as a sign among you. In the future, when your children ask you, 'What do these stones mean?' tell them that the flow of the Jordan was cut off before the ark of the covenant of the LORD. When it crossed the Jordan, the waters of the Jordan were cut off. These stones are to be a memorial to the people of Israel forever."

JOSHUA 4:5–7

It was one of the harder days Sharon and I had experienced as caregivers to Genevieve. It was the day the Alzheimer's had finally worked its destruction into the microscopic neuron of Genevieve's mind that contained the recognition of Sharon. Her name was now lost to Genevieve and with it all memory and recognition that Sharon was her daughter or someone to whom she had given life, identity, and being. There is no way to describe the pain and loss you feel when someone who has been that essential to the essence of your life has no memory of who or what you are. In some ways, it feels as though you are now lost because you have been lost to the person who has loved you so much and so well.

In the place of memory, recognition, and love there was only a blank expression in Genevieve's eyes. We called them "dead eyes" because there was simply no life left in there. But, of course, Genevieve was still alive and needed to be cared for properly.

It is difficult to care for people with whom there is no more emotional connection. You can be dedicated and committed, but emotion is one of the most important aspects of connection in human relationships. When it is gone, we often find ourselves just doing activities halfheartedly or not at all. People always marvel at how family members can leave their elderly loved ones in a facility of some type and never or seldom visit. I do not marvel and am not surprised. Most of these folks are good, well-intentioned people; they've just lost their emotional connection with their loved one.

So what do we do when the person we care for has no more emotion? I suggest something that is a difficult practice and not possible every day: we can regain our emotional connection by *remembering*. We remember the joy and connection when we were taught to ride a bicycle or tie our first tie. We remember the look of pride, joy, and relief when we told them the news of their grandchild. We remember the pain and sorrow they felt when their parents began to decline physically and eventually died. We remember their hard work, their laughter, their frustrations and anger, as well as their sacrifices and love. In other words, we connect with them emotionally by remembering the emotions of the past.

When I remember Genevieve's infectious laugh and how she used to read newspaper articles to me that she thought I'd be interested in, I smile. When I remember the way she cuddled my daughter the very first time she laid eyes on her, I am touched. And when I feel these emotions, I find that I am once again connected to Genevieve and able to care and relate to her in an effective way.

When the people of Israel crossed the Jordan River to enter the Promised Land, they set up stones to trigger memory. The stones were a way for the succeeding generations to emotionally connect with the past. That connection with the past allowed them to emotionally invest into the promise, commitment to, and care for the land. When we remember the lives of the people we care for—even if they are past the point of emotionally connecting with us—we can emotionally connect with them. This connection ties us together in the caregiving relationship and will make us more effective and caring. How far can this kind of emotion take us? To the place where we are effective and connected caregivers.

DAY 7

Morning Prayer

May We Make People Visible

"Everyone who exalts himself will be humbled, and he who humbles himself will be exalted."

LUKE 18:14

Joseph "John" Merrick, the Elephant Man, lived in nineteenth-century London and started his life largely invisible to the world. Born with a disease called neurofibromatosis, Merrick's bone and skin became twisted and grotesquely disfigured like heaps of stale jelly. After his mother died when he was very young, Merrick was cast aside by his family and eventually forced to earn his living as a "freak" in a circus sideshow. There he suffered the humiliation of being an object of people's revulsions and curiosity and was in many ways treated worse than an animal.

When Merrick became desperately ill and was left by his sideshow manager, he was taken to a hospital and cared for by a physician, Frederick Treves, whom he had met years earlier when Treves inquired about studying him medically. Merrick's plight and story became publicized, and eventually Queen Victoria herself championed the cause of the unfortunate man. He thrived under the care of the hospital and responded by reading, writing poetry, and constructing small models of buildings he saw from his window. The hospital eventually made Merrick a permanent resident, and he became a celebrity among London's high society, as visitors wished to rub elbows with the famous Elephant Man.

Very few of us care for someone with even half of the severe maladies that Merrick dealt with, but those who need care do share something with him, namely, the sense of being largely invisible to the rest of the world. The world is fascinated with glamour and glitz. We love the stories of the most talented as they compete for the prize on *American Idol*. We hunger for more details of the private lives of movie stars and their latest affairs, divorces, babies, and breakups. We seek the rich, well known, and beautiful in part because we want to become rich, well known, and beautiful ourselves.

But when you are in need of caregiving, the world tends to shy away. The world is embarrassed by the fact that a person cannot care for himself or herself. It shies away from need because it doesn't want to have to be responsible to meet a possible need. It is simply easier to pretend that a person who needs care doesn't really exist. Therefore, the person in need of care becomes invisible, and when he or she is invisible long enough, he or she starts to feel less than human. And whenever people feel less than human, it is because "normal" people have responded with disrespect, lack of care, or abuse. It is the plight of all who cannot care for themselves physically, financially, mentally, or emotionally. In short, they are often despised—and they disappear.

But Merrick did not remain invisible, in large part because he found first one person and then others who saw him for who he truly was—a human being. They gave him food and provided housing, care, and something absolutely essential to the human condition—respect. Merrick flourished not just because his sickness became better but primarily because his isolation from people's revulsion was removed.

Think of the many "invisibles" whom Jesus touched: a woman caught in adultery, a thief on a cross next to him, a tax collector with no true friend, a man blind at birth—just a few of the misfits who had emotional and physical maladies no one wanted to deal with because the need was too great and the mess would be overwhelming. But Jesus touched these invisible people and made them people once again. By the power of his presence and the promise of his care, he raised them to be on his level of importance.

We do not care for maladies and diseases; we care for people. When we remember how important people are to Jesus and how he made them human through respect, dignity, and care, we get a glimpse of how we can do the same. May we make the person for whom we give care visible and fully human by the way we give care this day.

Evening Reflection

There Is a Time

> *There is a time for everything …*
> *a time to weep and a time to laugh,*
> *a time to mourn and a time to dance.*

ECCLESIASTES 3:1, 4

One day I walked into a resident's room, and an awful stench ripped its way through my nostrils. After steadying myself a bit, I girded my will, took a deep breath, and went on a search for the source, amid the protests of a very sweet cognitively impaired woman. I found the source very quickly—a pile of used adult diapers in her bathroom. "I need those things for later," the woman protested.

Then there was the day my family went out to eat lunch at a restaurant. Genevieve was sitting at the table, unusually focused on the ketchup bottle. We kept wondering about her fascination, explaining, "It's ketchup, Genevieve. Do you want some on your food?" But she said nothing about it until we were ready to leave. Then she spoke up.

"I don't think it's right!" she protested. "They shouldn't charge you for that, because no one touched it at all." We reassured her that it was OK, that we *weren't* being charged, but she became aggressive as she struggled to take the ketchup along with her.

And then there was the day I was sitting at my desk in the personal care home when I heard an unmistakable "plop," like water dripping, in the dining room outside my office. I ignored it until another "plop" echoed in the empty room. I started looking around, suspecting some type of leak. Another "plop" sounded beside me, and I looked up at the open ceiling that stretched up to the third floor of the building. It had to be a leak.

I made my way up to the third-floor landing to get a closer look at the ceiling and track the source of the problem. Just as I reached the top of the stairs, I saw five-foot-tall, eighty-three-year-old Maria lean way over the railing and let a juicy mouthful of spit hurl out of her mouth, spiraling down to yet another giant "plop" in the dining room.

The fact is, I have a hundred stories that start with the line, "Then there was the day when …"—and like these three, they all make me laugh. Not just the kind of laugh that sneaks out when the corners of my mouth curl a bit. They make me close my eyes and let out a belly laugh. And I believe laughing *is* the correct response to these situations.

When you think about it, caregiving is an absurd job. The people we care for are infirmed in a variety of ways: some are unconscious or barely conscious and need help with every task; some are confused and make mental errors that require cleanup or hours to correct the problems; some are dying or deteriorating to the point where their body systems shut down and cannot be coaxed into functioning properly. But no matter the situations or ailments of the people for whom we care, they all have something in common: they are losing control, and so we step in to fill the gap. Some things we do are highly effective, but many are simply small fixes to problems that cannot be solved. The people we care for will eventually lose all control, and we will eventually lose the ability to control and help them.

Deterioration and eventual death are facts of life. In the wonderful poetry of Ecclesiastes 3, we are reminded that there is a time for everything. When I think of the days I mentioned above, I think of how funny we must look in trying to control life, and how inept our efforts are.

Sure, we can sit down and cry, but I certainly don't cry when I see a toddler stumble and fall when she tries to walk or when I see a preschooler spin around and around until dizziness overtakes him and he goes "plop." I don't cry when an adolescent takes on too much schoolwork and too many activities, yet confidently states, "I have plenty of time to get a job and get the rest I need." Instead, I smile and laugh because I know that in God's timing all will be well and that these young ones will learn.

That is how I look at caregiving. Our efforts look funny and are often misguided, but we will eventually learn. We will learn that we ultimately do not control our lives and that God will eventually take us and our charges by the hands and lead us to a perfected place in heaven.

There is a time to mourn a loss, especially in the deep pain of missing our loved one. But there also is a time to laugh at the strange efforts we make along the way of learning that we do not have control. And I'm quite convinced that in these times God chuckles along with us.

DAY 8

Morning Prayer

May I Be Committed to Communion

"I tell you the truth, unless you eat the flesh of the Son of Man and drink his blood, you have no life in you. Whoever eats my flesh and drinks my blood has eternal life, and I will raise him up at the last day. For my flesh is real food and my blood is real drink. Whoever eats my flesh and drinks my blood remains in me, and I in him. Just as the living Father sent me and I live because of the Father, so the one who feeds on me will live because of me."

JOHN 6:53–57

Jesus was a man who did not hesitate to say something disturbing in order to get his point across. When we traditionally think of "Communion," we think of a solemn and serious occasion in which we, usually as a congregation, take in the elements of bread and wine in "remembrance" of Jesus. We remember Jesus' sacrifice for us and the elements of grace he bestowed on us. Perhaps we remember to confess our sins and reaffirm our commitment to the living God. These things are good and proper, but as good as they are, I somehow feel that Jesus would have a word or two to say about what *communion* is really about.

Jesus was radical in the way he desired to commune with us. When he asked the disciples to follow him, they somehow knew that he was talking about a lifetime commitment to living differently. When he calls us to commune with him, he seems to make no hesitation that he intends us to take part in every aspect of the spiritual life. "Eat my flesh," he invites us. "Drink my blood."

47

All this flesh eating and blood drinking is disturbing stuff. It was disturbing to people when Jesus first said it, and many withdrew from him. Many, including the disciples, were tempted to leave. But there it is in plain and upfront words: "If you are going to be a part of me, you must make my essence your essence. You must consume my heart, my commitment, my love into your life. Like me, you must be willing to sacrifice yourself. You must suffer my indignations and pain. You must be called what I am called. And if you do, you will be a part of me and will have all the benefits of my kingdom and eternal life." He calls us, "Come, eat of my body and drink of my blood."

To commune with Jesus is very different from the idea of just participating in Communion. To commune means that we are willing to join every part of our beings to the being of Jesus. When I make the commitment to commune, it means that, at least at some level, I become the hands and feet of Jesus. When I give care to the person who needs me, will they see Jesus in me with a humble spirit that wants the best? Will my caregiving charge see in me the Jesus who wants nothing more in the world than to take away the pain and suffering he or she may feel? Will the person I care for see that I love with the sacrificial love of Jesus—a love that is more than willing to put his or her needs above my own? Will he or she see that I am meek, kind, peaceful, joyful, gentle, and disciplined? If I truly commune with the Son of God, then the answer will be yes, even though I do not reflect Jesus perfectly.

Jesus does not want caregiving believers who simply remember that he was a sacrificial and loving person; he wants caregiving believers who at their very core are connected to the living God and who are sacrificial and loving persons because that is what Jesus is and does.

As we begin this day, with all of the challenges of caregiving, Jesus is calling us to be committed to communion with him.

He reminds us that he is a part of everything we do in the day and that we are a part of him in every aspect of his kingdom to come. Let us not simply remember; let us commune. May we be committed to communion with the most loving and most sacrificial Jesus.

Evening Reflection

Jesus Knows Struggles and Sympathizes

We do not have a high priest who is unable to sympathize with our weaknesses, but we have one who has been tempted in every way, just as we are—yet was without sin. Let us then approach the throne of grace with confidence, so that we may receive mercy and find grace to help us in our time of need.

HEBREWS 4:15–16

John Adams and Thomas Jefferson, their political careers and competitive animosity long since behind them, seemingly willed themselves to stay alive until the fifty-year anniversary of the signing of the Declaration of Independence. Adams, however, had never quite lost his competitive envy for Jefferson's place in American history, having felt that his own contribution to the revolutionary fight had gone unnoticed. On July 4, 1826, a very sick and old Adams uttered his last words: "Thomas Jefferson lives."

He was wrong. Jefferson had died on the same anniversary of the famous signing—just hours earlier in the day. Obsessed with Jefferson's stature and the seemingly lukewarm esteem in which the nation held Adams, Adams let the discouragement over his place in history overshadow the important contribution he had made to the development of an entire nation.

So it is with many caregivers. At best, we serve in a job that has very little recognition and where the person we give care to may never get better. At worst, we may be giving care to someone who resents the efforts we make. They may become angry and constantly complain or attack our inadequacies. To make things worse, our siblings or family members may be aggressive and claim we are "control freaks"—or any of a hundred other insulting phrases.

It is easy to get discouraged and caught up in the idea that no one sees us as important or will remember our sacrifices. No one appreciates the disgusting messes we have cleaned up. No one realizes the important events in our own lives that we missed because we were giving care. No one imagines the indignities we have to swallow when others accuse us or attack us with insults about our effort. No one understands the sacrifices we have made and the cost to our own welfare.

There is one, however, who is the greatest of caregivers. He is an expert at cleaning up disgusting messes in our lives. He sympathizes with the reality of what we experience in that he lost his place of greatness. And he knows all about receiving insults and punishment when all he tried to do was love and serve. Jesus knows the complexities of our situations and indeed has set us where we are for a specific purpose.

Most likely, you did not choose to be a caregiver. It was a job forced on you because no one else was willing or able to serve. You may not even be very good at it. The point, however, is that you are where you are as a caregiver for however long God sees fit to use you there. It may not make sense to you, but God is at work in your discouragement with a specific purpose. What that purpose is about is yours to find.

Like John Adams, we can look at our current situation and sink into deep discouragement because no one understands or appreciates us. But no matter how we may be feeling, Jesus does understand and sympathize with our struggles to serve, show kindness, and make sense of why he has us in the situations in which we find ourselves. Jesus is willing and able to give us the grace needed to stay in there—no matter how difficult the circumstances—and keep on making our important contribution of loving others.

Morning Prayer

May I Look for Life's Surprises

"Blessed are your eyes because they see; and your ears because they hear. For I tell you the truth, many prophets and righteous men longed to see what you see but did not see it, and to hear what you hear but did not hear it."

MATTHEW 13:16–17

"If you hold each other close, things will be OK." If there was a saying by which Genevieve lived her life, it was this one—words communicating the reassuring power of family and intimacy. Now she was in her final days of a nine-year struggle with Alzheimer's disease. She was years past her ability to say words or complete sentences, yet in her comatose condition, she still delivered one more sweet surprise.

Sharon, her brother John, and I had gathered to help Genevieve cross the finish line of a tortuous, diseased life. As caregivers, Sharon and I had long since come to the place of peace of having said our good-byes and were comfortable that we didn't have to be present for her death. But when I knew death was very near, I went to sit with John for his mother's last moments. All morning as she labored hard to breathe, I thought each breath might be her last and was amazed at her ability to hold on. As we were sitting there, with Genevieve's death imminent, Sharon happened to call to check on her mother. "I think it will be within the hour," I said. I was surprised when Sharon said, "I do think I want to be there."

As was her habit in her mother's last few months, Sharon crawled into the bed with her mother, stroked her hair, and held her with a big hug across her middle. "I love you, Mom," she said as she pulled her mother close.

Holding his mother's hand on her other side, John said, "It's OK to let go, Mom. We'll be OK."

Sitting beside her pillow, I gently stroked her cheek and said, "It has been a tough road, but you have made it. We will see you in heaven."

Sharon added, "You will be free with your healed mind, and you'll be dancing in heaven."

John reaffirmed, "Yes."

And then Genevieve took her last three breaths: one breath, to hold the moment of having her children caress her; another breath, to drink in the reality of her lifelong lesson; and then one last half breath that did not get down to her lungs—just enough to taste for one last time the love that was in the room. Then she was gone, slipping out of our hands into the presence of the living God as easily as a raindrop gliding off of a flower petal.

Only then did I remember the lifelong lesson that Genevieve lived by: If you hold each other close, things will be OK. Somehow she had held on to get one more time of closeness so she would feel OK about leaving. Gentle. Peaceful. Dare I say it? Joyful. The one last surprise that Genevieve had in store was her ability to still teach us the lesson of her life and bring us together for one last hug.

We never know when these small teachable moments will come—times when we are surprised by how we can learn from the ones in our care. Even in situations where our loved ones appear to be totally dependent, they still very much possess a power to teach us. God still uses the relationship to teach us about truth, reality, and growth. They are dependent on us, but we are also dependent on them to teach us the lessons of living and loving. But of course, we will only learn if we have eyes to see and ears to hear. The lessons taught by the people we care for are subtle and most often taught in small moments and by nonverbal communication. It is the way the Spirit of God often teaches us—not by a blatant hammer over the head but a gentle direction dependent on our recognition.

Today, in my caregiving journey, I want to be teachable. I want to tune my ears and eyes to the surprises of growth. I desire to guard against becoming complacent in the teachable moments of the monotony of performing duties. I want to learn from my caregiving.

Evening Reflection

Who Will Leave a Monument?

"The King will reply, 'I tell you the truth, whatever you did for one of the least of these brothers of mine, you did for me.'"
MATTHEW 25:40

Abraham Lincoln spoke eloquently at the dedication ceremony of the cemetery at Gettysburg about the principles of freedom and the cause of democracy. At one point in his speech, he mentioned that while the world would little remember the ceremony, they would never forget the dedication and bravery of the men who fought and died on the great battlefield.

Like many, I have been to Gettysburg and found the area surrounded with monuments recognizing the individual sacrifices and marking the locations of the various regiments. I was touched deeply with "the feel" of the three days of war, when men struggled so gallantly among one another. I was awed by the courage it took to perform such great feats of defense and attack when the threat of death loomed so large. It was one of the most solemn reminders in my life that war is the ultimate travesty in the human struggle.

While it is so right for us to remember the brave, courageous, great, and successful through monuments, one has to wonder where the monuments are for all the great caregivers of the world. No one is going to rush out to name a park in your honor or erect a statue with a memorialized statement such as, "He or she gave impeccable care in the face of overwhelming work, financial, and family pressures." People will little remember the messes you've cleaned up, the nerves you've calmed, the patient service you've provided, the meals you've cooked, or the love you've shared. No one will immortalize your life through song or wish to live vicariously through you. So why would we dedicate our lives to a practice that is so little noticed and so unlikely to be remembered?

Essentially, we do what we do because the faithfulness of the act is remembered—not necessarily by people here on earth, but by our heavenly Father. In one of the most stirring passages in all of Scripture, Jesus tells the story of his coming into his glory, with the whole of creation set before him. At that moment, he will put those who belong to him on his right and turn away those who are on his left. He says to the ones on his right, "Come in and share my kingdom with me because I was hungry and thirsty and you fed me and gave me drink." He goes on to say that he was a sick stranger without clothes who needed care—and this group nursed him, greeted him, and clothed him. Confused, the righteous group protested that they had never seen Jesus hungry, thirsty, as a sick stranger in need of clothes and care. Jesus replied with words of hope for us caregivers: "I tell you the truth, whatever you did for one of the least of these brothers of mine, you did for me" (Matthew 25:40).

Jesus gives us the kind of assurance Abraham Lincoln gave to the men of Gettysburg. The world may forget our service as a caregiver, but Jesus will never forget. There is a monument reserved for us that recalls every selfless act, everything we missed out on in order to provide for someone else, every disgusting and unpleasant task we performed. The monument is in our eternal relationship with Jesus. When we did those things for the person we loved and cared for here on earth, we were, in fact, doing those things for Jesus.

It's as though Jesus is saying, "You were there to dress my wounds after I was beaten. You were there to clothe me when I hung naked on the cross. You were there to speak to me and comfort me during the long watch as death came over me." Jesus' assurance that our acts as caregivers will never be unnoticed or forgotten is one of the great comforts that gets us focused enough to keep on doing the job of caregiving. Let us always remember that he is watching and preparing the monument for us.

DAY 10

Morning Prayer

May I Never Be Alone

By the grace given me I say to every one of you:
Do not think of yourself more highly than you ought, but
rather think of yourself with sober judgment, in accordance
with the measure of faith God has given you.

ROMANS 12:3

Perhaps you are new at being a caregiver and have secret conversations with yourself in which you wonder if you are up to the challenge. At one time or another, all caregivers have this conversation with themselves—especially when they first started out. After all, there are many things to learn about just the practice of caregiving, like how to give medications, provide special diets, and formulate schedules. There are also the harder things to learn, like giving and receiving encouraging words, knowing when to be silent and when to listen, and caring for oneself.

There is no school to teach you how to be a caregiver, just as there's no school to teach you to be a parent. At least with parenting, the job starts off a little more simple and gets more complex as time goes on. With caregiving, however, you are typically thrown into the middle of the lake and must learn how to do caring while you are actually giving care. There are few apprenticeships, and usually the caregiving learning curve is very short indeed.

Of all the things to do when our competence is challenged, isolation is by far the worst choice. It is, however, what most caregivers do most often when they feel under the gun or at the end of their rope. Caregivers usually possess two characteristics that greatly contribute to the problem—characteristics most often considered strengths, but like any strength, when used inappropriately it becomes a weakness.

The first characteristic is hard work. Most of us consider this value one of our most tried-and-true allies. When things are tough, we simply convince ourselves to be tougher and to work harder. The second characteristic is control. Again, most caregivers I know are masters at keeping control of multiple schedules and are consummate multitaskers. But we know that our *perceived* control is never a reality, and when we try to control things too much, we frustrate the people around us and discourage ourselves. The truth is, when we are wondering if we are up to the task of caregiving, hard work and control are seldom our friends because most often they simply contribute further to our isolation.

The deep questioning that goes on inside of us as caregivers is actually the Holy Spirit notifying us of a special and precious truth—a truth that says, "This job of caregiving is too big for just one person. You will need physical help, emotional encouragement, and care and nurture for yourself."

You see, there are legions of caregivers in this country alone, and the number is growing every day. As unique as you think your situation is, I guarantee you that someone somewhere has been through the situation before. Connection with other caregivers provides us with mentoring from people who are familiar with our situation. Relationships with other caregivers help us know where the pitfalls in the process exist and how we can avoid those situations. But most of all, sharing with other caregivers gives us the encouragement and intimacy needed to let us know that people just like us can do this job successfully and ties us to a resource that fills our hearts instead of draining them.

God wants us connected in our times of distress and questioning. He doesn't want us to be isolated and controlling—to depend on the false belief that "we can handle it." May we strive to be connected with others in the caregiving community, and may we never be alone.

Evening Reflection

Justice Is Real; Grace Is Revealed

Now a righteousness from God, apart from law, has been made known, to which the Law and the Prophets testify. This righteousness from God comes through faith in Jesus Christ to all who believe. There is no difference, for all have sinned and fall short of the glory of God, and are justified freely by his grace through the redemption that came by Christ Jesus.

ROMANS 3:21–24

Commands, commands, commands. Sometimes there just seem to be too many commands. First, I have the Ten Commandments—four on keeping God first and foremost in my life, and six on how to live with my fellow humans. To keep us on our toes, we are reminded that our God is a jealous and awesome God: "Be careful not to forget the covenant of the LORD your God that he made with you; do not make for yourselves an idol in the form of anything the LORD your God has forbidden. For the LORD your God is a consuming fire, a jealous God" (Deuteronomy 4:23–24).

Then there's Jesus, who says that if I really love him, I will keep his commands (John 14:15). And what is his take on the commandments? Boiled down, it's this: "'Love the Lord your

God with all your heart and with all your soul and with all your mind.' This is the first and greatest commandment. And the second is like it: 'Love your neighbor as yourself' " (Matthew 22:37–39).

Thanks a lot, Jesus! So all I have to do to fulfill the Law and the Prophets is give my heart, commitment, and will to God and love people as I would want to be loved.

Both Old and New Testaments underscore this basic fact: the way we live really does matter to God. And because he is just, he expects us to strive to obey his commandments perfectly. But we are far from perfect. Daily, I face the temptation of seeking a newer car, more money, or more success. There are days when I am a complete disaster at the job of loving my neighbor as myself. Most days, the only words I have in common with that well-known phrase is "loving" and "myself."

The job of caregiving does little to help the situation. Most of the time I sense that my role as a caregiver has totally squeezed out my relationship with God, and all he can possibly get from me are a few scraps and leftovers of time. Sometimes I'm racked with guilt because I carry around anger or frustration that my siblings aren't helping me enough with caregiving or that the person I'm caring for is just not cooperating. If justice is real, then truly it is God's mercy that I have not been consumed long ago!

Which is precisely the point: I fall far short of the expectation of the commandments. I am not made OK by the fact that I try hard to obey the commandments. I am not made OK by the fact that I try to do good things by giving care to someone who really needs me. I am OK because Jesus makes up for my lacking. He takes the heat for my failures and sin. He completes me because he chose to give grace that connected me in relationship with God.

Whenever I am focused on my shortcomings and failures as a man and a caregiver, I usually become aware that I am not matching up to the two greatest commandments. It does motivate me to do better—at least somewhat. But when I become aware of the grace of Jesus Christ and the price he paid to bring me into right relationship with God, I am motivated much more.

I know that Jesus is my brother in striving with me and encouraging me toward more godly responses and love. Justice is real, and it is a motivator because fear and guilt point to what needs to be corrected. But when grace is revealed, thankfulness and encouragement set us on the path toward living differently. Commandments are good and clear, but we do better in living godly lives under grace.

DAY 11

Morning Prayer

May I Love with the Deepest Love

Dear friends, since God so loved us, we also ought to love one another. No one has ever seen God; but if we love one another, God lives in us and his love is made complete in us.

1 JOHN 4:11–12

I am a backyard astronomer, which means I'm out in the middle of the night when most of the sane world is asleep. I love many things about the night sky, but nothing excites me more than comets. As a child, reading about Halley's Comet ignited my whole interest in astronomy, and I've had the wonderful pleasure of viewing many comets as an adult. I love how the hazy ball with indistinct edges gives way to a gentle tail that stretches millions of miles across the night sky. The whole reason a comet is beautiful, however, is the fact that it is losing part of itself every time it approaches the sun. Dust and ice are ripped away from the comet by the sun's solar wind, and this illuminated trail of "comet stuff" is what we see as the spectacular tail. Each suicidal plunge the comet takes to the sun during its orbit costs the orb more and more of itself.

And so it is with loving someone else. The love—true *agape* love—that is found in the Scripture is not simply unconditional acceptance. Agape love is self-sacrificing and altruistic. It is the kind of love that doesn't just look out for the other guy first; it *only* looks out for the other guy. Of course, we see this kind of love in the most pristine form when we see Jesus taking on the burden of our sins and experiencing the pain and punishment that should have been meted out to us: "This is how God showed his love among us: He sent his one and only Son into the world that we might live through him. This is love: not that we loved God, but that he loved us and sent his Son as an atoning sacrifice for our sins" (1 John 4:9–10).

Sacrifice, atonement—these are aspects of Christ's agape love for humanity, and it is a love that always costs something. In order to plunge himself toward a loving relationship with us, he gave of himself and left parts of himself behind for our sakes.

Caregiving gives us the same kind of opportunities. When we give of ourselves, there is no expectation we will ever be paid back. The kind of care we give often does nothing to rehabilitate or help the person get better. Most times, our care is given to a loved one who will continue to be in bad shape or will worsen over time. These facts are what make our love so close to agape love. It is love that cannot be returned to us in the same way we gave it. It is love that is totally focused on the person we care for. It is, in short, the deepest kind of love we can experience and the kind most closely aligned with the way we are loved by Christ.

This kind of love costs us something. It may cost us part of our own health. It will likely cost us a good part of our time and economic well-being. It will cost us some of our individual hopes and dreams as we put more priority on caregiving than on driving ourselves toward success. As these parts are lost to us, they likely come off for good, and we leave them behind.

But let us take heart and remember the comet. Just as the comet leaves part of itself behind to give a wonderful and awesome show, so we lose part of ourselves for the sake of demonstrating a beautiful metaphor of how to love unselfishly for the good of another. May I love with the deepest kind of love for the one I give care to—the same kind of love that Christ gives to me.

Evening Reflection

To Be Truly Sanctified

> *"Sanctify them by the truth; your word is truth."*
> JOHN 17:17

S*anctification*. It's one of those big theological words we hear when we hang around churches and Bible studies long enough. But do we really know what it means? Perhaps you heard from your Sunday school teachers that *sanctify* means "to set apart, consecrate, or make holy." While accurate, those words never meant much to me.

When I asked a friend what *sanctify* meant to him, he pointed to a chair and went over and sat down. He said, "I am sanctifying the chair. In other words, to sanctify means that something is utilized perfectly and for the exact reason it was created."

This definition makes a lot of practical sense to me. When we are in the process of being sanctified as the Scriptures talk about, it means we are engaged in a step-by-step process to become exactly what we are created for in the original plan. And what is that plan? As I understand it as a Christian, it is, as the Westminster Catechism puts it, "to glorify God and enjoy him forever."

We are created for relationship in general and specifically for relationship with God. God is the creator, so it is right for us to have the place to love him, glorify him, and enjoy the fruit of the relationship forever. The apostle Paul taught, "We, who with unveiled faces all reflect the Lord's glory, are being transformed into his likeness with ever-increasing glory, which comes from the Lord, who is the Spirit" (2 Corinthians 3:18).

To put these ideas together, we are being perfected into our original purpose, which is to relate to God as created beings who glorify him and enjoy him. It is a wonderful picture to be fully restored to being with God in the way that only Adam and Eve knew before sin—always open, always in awe, and always in the comfort, desire, and love of the God of the universe. But the process isn't immediate and takes a lot of time.

So what does this have to do with slinging out the hard work of caregiving day in and day out? In actuality, our service, hard times, easy times, and trials are all part of God's working out of sanctification in us. God isn't just doling out circumstances to us in a haphazard way and is certainly not about the practice of punishing us. He is in the process of using our circumstances, people, and his word to work out this process of making us into persons who can perfectly fulfill our original purpose.

Since we are caregivers, we can assume that God is using our caregiving in this time and this place in order to work out the essence of godliness in us. It is no surprise. The apostle James writes, "Consider it pure joy, my brothers, whenever you face trials of many kinds, because you know that the testing of your faith develops perseverance. Perseverance must finish its work so that you may be mature and complete, not lacking anything" (James 1:2–4).

You feel put-upon by the responsibilities that press you to your limit? You are being sanctified. You feel impatient because the person you care for is uncooperative or manipulative? You are being sanctified. You deeply resent that the life you thought you'd have is being taken away? You are being sanctified. Don't be discouraged, for sanctification is a promise that will be accomplished as surely as birth and resurrection are accomplished. But if you're wondering what God is doing in all of your trials, challenges, and travails, be of good cheer. The King is preparing you to be used exactly for the purpose for which you were made.

DAY 12

Morning Prayer

May I Be Weak to Be Strong

He said to me, "My grace is sufficient for you, for my power is made perfect in weakness." Therefore I will boast all the more gladly about my weaknesses, so that Christ's power may rest on me. That is why, for Christ's sake, I delight in weaknesses, in insults, in hardships, in persecutions, in difficulties. For when I am weak, then I am strong.

2 CORINTHIANS 12:9–10

It must have been a stirring, yet slightly absurd, scene. The elderly Joshua and the people were going about the job of conquering and dividing the Promised Land. Joshua's old friend Caleb, the other faithful spy among the twelve sent to scout the "land flowing with milk and honey" (Exodus 3:8), came to Joshua to ask for his portion, as promised by Moses as a reward for his faithful service. Perhaps you remember the story. Joshua and Caleb had reasoned that if God was with them, then God would defeat their enemies and the land would be theirs. But the other ten spies had thought differently. They saw things only with their eyes instead of with the faith of their hearts, reporting that the Promised Land was inhabited by giants and that the people of Israel would be like grasshoppers trying to fight this mighty force (Numbers 13:31–33). The majority won the day, and as a result, God caused the people to wander until a whole generation died out.

Now, forty-five years later, Caleb is getting his turn to name the section of land he wanted to claim as his own. He steps forward and declares, "Just as the LORD promised, he has kept me alive for forty-five years since the time he said this to Moses, while Israel moved about in the desert. So here I am today, eighty-five years old! I am still as strong today as the day Moses sent me out: I'm just as vigorous to go out to battle now as I was then. Now give me this hill country that the LORD promised me that day" (Joshua 14:10–12).

Yes, the scene and statement were stirring—but a little absurd. Can you imagine a small, frail eighty-five-year-old stating that he was ready to go out to battle and conquer giants? This is a grasshopper ready to strike back with a vengeance!

While it may be true that God had kept Caleb strong and vigorous through miraculous means, I prefer to think not. I think Caleb realized that when he was forty, he was no more capable of defeating the giants than at the age of eighty-five. I believe Caleb knew it was God who would make him capable of taking the land. It was not Caleb's strength but the strength of the Lord that would win the day. Very simply, Caleb knew that in his own physical weakness, he was strong physically in the Lord.

How we caregivers need this message! When someone depends on us for basic things such as feeding, bathing, and shelter, we begin to think we must be strong for their sake. We come to believe that if we don't show that we are a solid rock, then somehow the person we care for will feel frightened and anxious. But the simple truth is that we do not have the strength solely in ourselves to do this job of caregiving. We need God's guidance on what needs to be done next. We need God's patience in realizing that the person we care for is a learning and growing individual who needs time and space to grow. We need God's sustaining love and connection when we feel alone and have no one to turn to in our need. We need God in our caregiving efforts.

As I begin each day, I want to remember that I need God. I want to remember to be willing to be weak and to acknowledge what I cannot do, so that the power of God in me can be made complete. I want to be humble enough to acknowledge my dependence on the Creator and Sustainer for both the simple and complicated things that come with caregiving. I want the person I care for to clearly see that I do not have it all under control, but that I depend on a God whom I trust *does* have things under control. May I be weak, so that the strength of God can shine through me and encourage others.

Evening Reflection

Running the Bobsled

> *Shout for joy to the LORD, all the earth,*
> *burst into jubilant song with music;*
> *make music to the LORD with the harp,*
> *with the harp and the sound of singing,*
> *with trumpets and the blast of the ram's horn —*
> *shout for joy before the LORD, the King.*

PSALM 98:4–6

I am a bobsledder — sort of. On a trip to Park Cities, Utah, during the summer before the Winter Olympics, I had a unique opportunity. If I passed it up, I knew I'd regret if for the rest of my life. So I ponied up $175 of my hard-earned cash to ride behind an Olympic bobsled driver.

I was shocked at how long it took three fat guys — one of them being me — to cram into the tiny, narrow space of a four-man bobsled. When one of the guys asked the driver if we were going to get a running start, he said, "No, it would be hard to get the sled back up here after you guys didn't make it in." So the driver gently pushed us off and then jumped in.

"Not a very glorified beginning," I thought to myself, but things soon changed as we started banking the curves. Nothing I write here can adequately describe what it's like to have four G's push you down perfectly still as you zoom through a curve close to the ground going somewhere in the neighborhood of eighty miles an hour. It was at once terrifying and exhilarating. And it was *so* cool.

One of the coolest things about it, however, is that the bobsled run took me to a whole new place, far away from the cares and worries of everyday life. It was a place where I had moments of pure joy and exuberance that have lasted me for years. On the one hand, the fifty-five-second ride was a waste of my money; on the other hand, it was a priceless experience.

When was the last time you did something that put you in this place of pure joy and exhilaration? Caregivers often have the reputation of going by the book—being cautious and scheduled. We have to be. Much of what we call "normal" depends on us learning how to manage difficult situations and struggle to control random occurrences and accidents. But really, don't you just wish you could let your hair down for a few crazy moments and hurl yourself down the bobsled run?

For you it may be a spur-of-the-moment trip, spending money on an extravagance you'd normally never take, getting a manicure or pedicure at a spa, or choosing one of a hundred recreational activities. But whatever it is, there's something out there with your name on it, calling you out of your mundane and managed life to do something spontaneous and joyful.

Most will look at this idea as good common sense. We need escape every now and again. But others will ask the question,

"Is letting our hair down a biblical idea?" I think so, because I believe that joy is a biblical concept. It is listed prominently among the fruit of the Spirit that should be representative of Christian character. With joy, we experience such excitement and enthusiasm that we are removed from whatever current burden we bear or heavy circumstance we face. Real joy is more than mere happiness. Joy focuses on all that is good, lovely, pure, and energizing. When we experience something joyful, we can't help but smile.

When we are given moments away from the monotony of controlled caregiving, we have the opportunity to feel the joy that releases us from the chains that can drag us into negativity and despair. And when we experience that kind of joy, we will find ourselves turning our thoughts, our thankfulness, and our praises to the God who made us with the ability to know such pleasure. If God created us in such a way that we can experience joy, then we should certainly take a little time to develop this beautiful fruit and feeling in our lives.

DAY 13

Morning Prayer

May I Take Care of Myself

*"I have had enough, LORD," [Elijah] said. "Take my life;
I am no better than my ancestors."*

1 KINGS 19:4

Desperate. That's what it feels like at times to be a caregiver.
Like a dead car battery that only has enough juice to give one
pitiful groan when the key is turned, we get to the end of our
rope physically, emotionally, mentally, and spiritually. There is
simply nothing left in us any longer, as though we've had all
of our energy zapped out of us and we've been put in the spin
cycle of a caregiving washing machine that makes sure all of our
resources are hurled out.

This kind of desperate, end-of-the-rope feeling can happen
in many ways. Sometimes it is when our loved one goes through
a particularly taxing few weeks of being in the hospital. The
fragmented and fragile schedule we've worked so hard to string
together is decimated by the immediate needs of running tests,
waiting for results, and keeping a watchful eye at the hospital
bedside. Perhaps we get the desperate, drained feeling when we
have worked to be faithful to our task of caregiving, only to be
criticized or unappreciated by family members or the one for
whom we provide so much care. Or maybe it's because we have
exhausted all of our resources through the relentless day-in and
day-out of routine, in which we give more to someone else than
we take from God, others, and our own nurture. Whatever the

reason, it is an awful feeling, one in which we lose hope that we will ever feel good or energized again.

Such was the case when Elijah received a messenger from Jezebel. Elijah had just witnessed the sacrifice at Mount Carmel, where the prophets of the false god Baal had been consumed. While this should have been a "Super Bowl" winning moment for Elijah, it laid him low because Jezebel was determined to hunt him down and kill him. Simply stated, he ran away and gave up: "I have had enough, LORD," he said. "Take my life" (1 Kings 19:4). Like caregivers who reach the end of their emotional and physical strength, Elijah was totally and utterly spent.

The Bible tells us that God cared for Elijah in very practical ways. Elijah went to sleep. After he had rested, he ate food provided by an angel. Then he went to sleep and ate again. With the strength gained from food and rest, Elijah went out to seek the Lord and tell him how tired and alone he felt from doing what he had told him to do.

God then showed Elijah some of his great power:

> Then a great and powerful wind tore the mountains apart and shattered the rocks before the LORD, but the LORD was not in the wind. After the wind there was an earthquake, but the LORD was not in the earthquake. After the earthquake came a fire, but the LORD was not in the fire. And after the fire came a gentle whisper. When Elijah heard it, he pulled his cloak over his face and went out and stood at the mouth of the cave.

> 1 KINGS 19:11–13

We really don't know what the whisper was, but surely it was some kind of assurance such as, "I am powerful; you are weak. I am with you always."

We all reach the end of our resources. What do we need? We need restful sleep, good food, and the spiritual assurance that we are not alone. In other words, we need to take care of ourselves. There is much work to be done. There are prophets of Baal to be slain; evil kings and their wives need to be dealt with. The complicated and tiring work of caring for our loved one calls us. We cannot accomplish the mighty tasks ahead of us this day unless we take care of ourselves both physically and spiritually. For surely if we go down in a heap because we are too tired, undernourished, or depressed, there will be no one to carry out the necessary work.

Today may I be willing to take care of myself. God is with us just as much when we engage in caring for ourselves as he is when we love and care for someone else.

Evening Reflection

The Practice of Peace

"Peace I leave with you; my peace I give you. I do not give to you as the world gives. Do not let your hearts be troubled and do not be afraid."

JOHN 14:27

During my generation, the 1960s, the word *peace* was, of all things, a battle cry. Peace became the symbol of those who wanted an end to the war in Vietnam and became a greeting, farewell, and affectionate response all rolled into one. We used the word a lot.

Jesus also used the word a lot, and to him it meant two seemingly contradictory things. At one point he said, "Do you think I came to bring peace on earth? No, I tell you, but division" (Luke 12:51). Jesus makes clear that his ministry will bring about strife in households, as some family members believe in him and others oppose him.

On the other hand, Jesus clearly states that he is a bringer of peace. In one of the most beautiful and most quoted passages of the Gospels, he says, "Peace I leave with you; my peace I give you. I do not give to you as the world gives. Do not let your hearts be troubled and do not be afraid" (John 14:27). Here Jesus reassures us that he will always be with us through the presence of the Holy Spirit.

Those who practice peacemaking are blessed, according to the Sermon on the Mount (Matthew 5:9), and peace is a fruit of the Spirit (Galatians 5:22). But there is a practical truth that Luke 12:51 and John 14:27 spell out for us in our work as caregivers. First, there is the truth about power. Peace disappears when one party seeks power instead of peace. Why is there envy, strife, misunderstanding in relationships that escalate into harsh words, emotional cutoffs, and eventual retaliation and hatred? Simply stated, it is because I want my way. I want you to do things my way, see things my way, or feel things my way. If you don't, I will pull out a variety of power tricks such as anger, manipulation, threats, coercion, or my brute physical strength.

Through the years I've seen many caregiving relationships. It is often assumed that because the person being cared for is in need of a caregiver, they have no power. Nothing could be further from the truth. Power tricks are used by caregiver and care receiver both. If we are to practice peace and be peacemakers, we must be committed to not seeking power ourselves and to avoiding power struggles. When power struggles occur in the caregiving relationship, there will be a winner and a loser in the issue, but both parties will suffer emotionally and spiritually because of the battle. There are boundaries to be drawn in the caregiving relationship to protect individuals, but never should these boundaries be drawn out of the power tricks of anger, manipulation, threats, and coercion.

But it does take both caregiver and care receiver to disengage from the power battle, and the truth is that sometimes even when the caregiver disengages and seeks peace, the care receiver will continue employing the same tricks. Can we as caregivers still practice peace? The answer is a resounding yes. We can still hold to the practice of peace by remembering the second scriptural teaching. Jesus is with us in our endeavors to disengage from any power struggle that exists. We can serve and be clear with our boundaries while being willing to connect to the living God. And because of Jesus, the living God assures us that no power struggle exists in our relationship with him and that one day soon all the struggles with power in this world will be over.

Is this kind of peace appeasement? I don't think so. I think this kind of peace is an acknowledgment that most of the battles we engage in with the person we care for are really not important when we take an eternal view. It is a choice on our part, therefore, to be more connected to the eternal peace of life than the temporal power of the moment. May we in our caregiving be about the practice of peace. May we be peacemakers in our caregiving relationships. May we seek the peace that Jesus gives through our eternal relationship with him.

DAY 14

Morning Prayer

May I Look for Support

> *If one part suffers, every part suffers with it; if one part is honored, every part rejoices with it. Now you are the body of Christ, and each one of you is a part of it.*
>
> 1 CORINTHIANS 12:26–27

Mary Jane had a mental illness. Her illness had been a problem even before the slow drip of dementia began to drain away her logic and memory. Mary Jane was a hoarder—one who exhibited the kind of obsessive-compulsive behavior that is afraid to throw anything out because it might be of use later on or be valuable in some way.

When her son invited me to her one-bedroom apartment, I could hardly believe my eyes. Newspapers, boxes, trash bags, clothes, dishes, and just plain junk were stacked in huge heaps to the ceiling. There was no room to move, just a tiny trail to squeeze through sideways on the way to the kitchen. And the kitchen? Putrid garbage was packed in open bags where cockroaches would scatter with any movement. From what I could tell, every dish in the house had been used and was stacked in the sink. I had no idea how anyone would know where to begin to clean such a stack. Dust caked everything, and a musty stench of dirt, rotten food, and vermin droppings wafted through the air.

Yes, it was a mess—one her son was desperate to correct. He tried to get a handle on her financial situation and help her with her bills, only to get a resolute declaration from Mary Jane:

"I am perfectly capable." He wanted to get medical and psychological help, but she refused. He worked to get her untenable living situation corrected, to which she angrily proclaimed, "It's my house and I can take care of it myself." Sadly, I couldn't be of any help, and Mary Jane's son was left to see his mother suffer until the weight of her own incompetence crashed down around her.

The court eventually appointed the son as guardian, but only after she had lost most of her financial resources, been evicted from her apartment, and squandered most of her mental faculties to the point where she was unable to make any significant emotional connection to her son except to be angry at "this person" who had taken over her life. A sad end indeed for everyone concerned.

But how often do we caregivers make the same kinds of proclamations to those around us? We live in a society that prides itself on individuality and self-competency. How many times do we caregivers refuse the help of others who see that we are tired, worn down, stretched financially, or emotionally empty? Research clearly tells us that those who have the job of caregiving experience more depression and financial distress, are in poorer physical health, and have more relational dissatisfaction than the rest of the population. Yet how many times do we caregivers refuse help?

A caring couple sees that we need to get away for the weekend with our spouse, but we reason that letting someone else come in and teaching them what needs to be done would be more trouble than it's worth. Our friends see us neglect our own physical health and try to offer respite, but we reason that we'll just catch a nap when our loved one is resting. Family members offer to help us with our problems, but we often take offense, believing that they are being critical of us. In short, sometimes we aren't much different from Mary Jane. We hoard and hold on to our problems and burdens and proclaim, "I can do it myself!"

We cannot. God, in his infinite wisdom, made us to be interdependent. As individuals, but especially as caregivers, we need others to support and care for us as we carry out this difficult task. We are no more competent to do the job of caregiving alone than Mary Jane was competent to take care of her issues alone. As Paul reminds us, "If one part suffers, every part suffers with it; if one part is honored, every part rejoices with it. Now you are the body of Christ, and each one of you is a part of it" (1 Corinthians 12:26–27).

In all I do as a caregiver, may I be willing to allow others to provide the support and care I need to remain active and vital in the body of Christ. May I look for the support, and may I accept it.

Evening Reflection

The Truth about Infirmity

Carry each other's burdens, and in this
way you will fulfill the law of Christ.

GALATIANS 6:2

No one likes to be infirm. Whether we are sick, diseased, or disabled, infirmity is a constant reminder that we lack something and that we cannot perform up to par.

Franklin Roosevelt was infirm most of his adult life from polio, which left him crippled in his legs. But Roosevelt, owing to the lack of understanding and acceptance of his day, chose to hide his infirmity. He did his best to hide the painful and ugly braces he would have to wear in order to do a form of walking he called "stumping." He was seldom photographed in his wheelchair and was often "pre-seated" for special events and meetings. He simply hated the fact that he could not walk without assistance and assumed that most people who were "normal" would despise his infirmity also.

Most of us who are caregivers, however, know about infirmities. We see that in truth, infirmities usually bring us together. Take Tom and Anne, for example, a couple who had been married fifty-seven years. Tom, in the moderate stages of Alzheimer's, had difficulty remembering anything for more than a few minutes at a time. Anne had a mind as sharp as a razor, but she could barely walk because of her advanced osteoporosis.

Every morning, you would see their teamwork in action. Anne would tell Tom to get two eggs from the refrigerator. Tom would comply. She would tell him to get the pan from the cabinet. Tom would comply. She would instruct him on turning on the stovetop. Step by step, with Anne's mind and Tom's mobility, the couple would be eating breakfast within a half hour. You see, the couple actually *bore* each other's infirmities. Tom bore what Anne could not do and actually walked and cooked for both. Anne bore the work of thinking out things, not only for herself, but also for Tom. By bearing each other's infirmities, they were actually able to redeem one another and concentrate on the work of functioning independently.

The truth about infirmities is that all of us have something wrong with us. I may have a sharp mind and be able to take care of myself and others physically, but it doesn't mean that I don't have things wrong with me. I struggle emotionally with being too negative, which at times can drag me into the depths of depression. I tend to focus too much on getting tasks and work accomplished instead of on making intimate connections. The person I care for has to put up with or bear these infirmities on my behalf. I may do lifting, cleaning, and planning, but the person I care for must look out to encourage me and help me focus on being positive.

We won't always bear each other's infirmities perfectly. Sometimes I will drop the ball, and the bath won't get done or a mess will stay around too long. Sometimes my caregiving charge himself or herself will be depressed. But the fact remains that as a caregiver, I am not just taking care of problems, but instead I am functioning as part of a team that bears infirmities so that we may both be closer to normal.

We may not bear infirmities perfectly, but there is another member in the caregiving team who *is* able to do the job completely and perfectly. Isaiah writes of him, "Surely he took up our infirmities and carried our sorrows, yet we considered him stricken by God, smitten by him, and afflicted" (Isaiah 53:4). Jesus Christ himself bears our infirmities, as well as the infirmities of our caregiving charge. Together, Jesus, caregiver, and the one receiving care complete a trinity of functioning that moves us toward completion and wholeness.

DAY 15

Morning Prayer

May I Be a Long-Haul Caregiver

*The Holy Spirit warns me that ... hardships are facing me.
However, I consider my life worth nothing to me, if only I may
finish the race and complete the task the Lord Jesus has given me.*

ACTS 20:23–24

On one of my trips to teach in Germany, I went to the city of
Ulm, where the tallest cathedral in Europe is located. Unwilling
to let my chance for a spectacular view go to waste, I started
climbing the endless circular staircase on the way to the top of
one of the spires.

Although I had no idea how many steps there were, I found
a gauge that would tell me how I was doing. You see, where the
staircase started, the area was totally trashed. Cigarette butts and
empty soda containers were everywhere. It was trashy like this
for about four stories, until there was an awful stench of where
people's stomachs had given up their last full measure. Obviously, the folks who left their lunch didn't quite have the right
stuff for the long haul.

After holding my breath and making it past this obstacle
course, I started having to dodge people themselves. Every fifteen or so steps, there would be a person sitting on the staircase,
gasping for air and trying to recapture the precious strength to
proceed. "Not a finisher," I'd say to myself.

But as I neared the top, I saw by far the ugliest sight of my
long climb. Individuals had taken markers, rocks, and even tools

to make a monument to themselves. There were rows and rows of names, dates, and sayings. Too tired to make it to the top, they took to cheating the process in an attempt to make their efforts worth something.

How sad! Here was this lovely cathedral, a monument to the years of dedication and love people felt toward God and service, defaced with others' vain effort to leave a mark to say "I was here." The profound thing was that I did not remember a single name or date. None of those people will be remembered by their childish vandalism. All it did was distract me from the pristine beauty of the true monument.

When I reached the top and gazed out over the wonderful view of the wide expanse of the city, however, not even the ugliness I'd encountered on my way up could overcome my awe. What the generations of caring and trustworthy people had produced in their reverence toward God was truly inspiring.

Caregiving is indeed a long climb. Along the way we will encounter many who are not in the kind of shape that allows them to make such a climb. We will see others who put out the effort, only to give up quickly because they don't have the necessary stamina. We will eventually reach a point in ourselves where we feel as though we can give no more. At that point we are tempted to scratch our names on the wall and say, "That surely is good enough. I can go no further." We want to leave our high-water mark and retreat from the work we have endured. But to be a long-haul caregiver, we must continue.

There is no doubt in my mind that God honors any work we do in caring for another. When we, by reasons of our own health limitations or family obligations, have to hand the task to someone else, God takes joy in our service and efforts. But I also have no doubt that God has special regard for those who were able to start the task and continue all the way to completion—to that day when either we or our loved ones go to be with the Lord.

God loves unselfish service, but I believe he has a special place in his love for finishers—those who endured the long climb as long-haul caregivers. Like Paul, may we be able to proclaim, "I have fought the good fight, I have finished the race, I have kept the faith. Now there is in store for me the crown of righteousness, which the Lord ... will award to me" (2 Timothy 4:7–8). At the end, we can take in the full joy and view of a life given to service and hear the words, "Well done, good and faithful servant" (Matthew 25:21).

In all my caregiving, may I have the attitude of a long-haul caregiver. Each day when I awake and with each new challenge I face, may I remember that God rejoices in my unselfish love from the beginning of the job through all the difficulties and challenges and on to the very end, when the caregiving job is over.

Evening Reflection

Keeping Yourself Healthy

Be very careful, then, how you live—not as unwise but as wise,
making the most of every opportunity, because the days are evil.
Therefore do not be foolish, but understand what the Lord's will is.

EPHESIANS 5:15–17

In actuality, it was such a foolish thing. George Washington was in his sixties, retired from the presidency—a vital and active man. He had insisted, as was his custom, to ride out in the cold, damp weather to check on the work at his plantation. Though the weather turned even bitterer, he continued his rounds until later in the evening.

After arriving back at his Mount Vernon home later than usual, he refused to keep his guests waiting any longer for dinner and entertained and ate in his damp clothes. The next morning, though he felt under the weather with a sore throat, he complicated his folly by deciding to again make rounds through the plantation in the frigid cold. Within the week, the "Father of Our Country" was dead—primarily out of his own foolishness and unwillingness to take care of himself.

What was the critical juncture in Washington's decision-making process? It was the point when he convinced himself it was more important to put himself at risk than to inconvenience others.

Caregivers are notorious for these types of foolish decisions. It is as though we become so good at taking care of others and so selfless in our love that we really start to believe there's nothing we can't do or handle. This is especially true when it comes to our own health. We may have a cold or the flu, but we convince ourselves it's a greater hassle to call in another family member to do the caregiving or it's too intrusive into other people's lives. So we press on and do the caregiving ourselves. We have an ache or pain we would never leave unaddressed for the person we care for, but we put off our own visit to the doctor because we just don't have time to take off.

George Washington was a great man, but he did a foolish thing that resulted in his death. You may be a great and unselfish caregiver, but don't think you aren't capable of the same foolish behavior that can result in tragic consequences. I have seen caregivers ignore their own blood pressure or diabetes issues only to have strokes or lose limbs to amputations. I have seen caregivers put off visits to the doctor for simple skin problems that resulted in terminal cancers. And I have seen caregivers die from pneumonia because they kept going long after the time when they should have been on bed rest and antibiotics.

Eating right, sleeping well, and getting the proper encouragement are just part of caring for yourself. The most essential item is setting the proper boundaries and getting the treatment you need for yourself when you are in need. If you are somehow under the illusion that you are the indispensable caregiver and that things just cannot operate without you, let me assure you that things *will* operate without you if you become incapacitated or die.

What is the alternative to making the foolish choice of not caring for yourself? It may be you'll have to call friends or family members to take your place in the caregiving job as you get the treatment you need. It may mean you'll have to hire temporary caregiving help. Sometimes it may even mean that the person you care for has to adjust to doing without some nonessential activities for a time.

You will fight this idea. You will say that other people are too busy to step in to relieve you, or that you're really not sick enough to require time off. You'll claim you don't have the available funds to hire caregiving help. You'll say you can't let your loved one go without these customary activities. And what you'll be saying is that it's more important to put yourself at risk than to inconvenience others. There is a fine line between being loving, humble, and sacrificial and just plain being foolish.

DAY 16

Morning Prayer

May I Remember the Great and the Good

*By him all things were created: things in heaven and on earth,
visible and invisible, whether thrones or powers or rulers or
authorities; all things were created by him and for him.*

COLOSSIANS 1:16

When I was a young boy, our house was about a block from
a vast open field of land where we were free to have our ball
games, play wars, and races. But the far end of the field posed
a great challenge. There stood two empty railroad boxcars, end
to end—with the wheels removed—which had probably been
used for storage at one time. The challenge for all of the boys in
the neighborhood was to climb on top of those boxcars. Why?
No particular reason, except we were ambitious and none of us
had yet accomplished the feat.

Finally one day, six of us toted ropes and ladders over to
the site to conquer the boxcars once and for all. We worked,
struggled, and wrestled every which way to get to the top, but
there was nothing to tie our ropes to and our ladders were too
short.

It was a hot day, and so about noon we nestled into a shady
nook by the boxcars. As we sat, one boy handled his nervous
energy by spreading his hands between the boxcars and swing-
ing his feet. Then, in one brilliant moment, he spread his feet
between the boxcars. It suddenly dawned on us that if we pressed
our hands and feet spread-eagle style to get leverage, we'd be

able to make the climb. Within minutes, all six of us were sitting on top of the boxcars taking in the view. We couldn't have accomplished the feat by concentrating the effort on one car; we had to learn to press ourselves against and between the two.

Life in general—and the task of caregiving in particular—presents us with enormous, difficult tasks and goals. Our goal is to live our lives in a godly manner that mimics the servanthood and love demonstrated by Jesus. We resonate with the heavenly idea that one day there will be no more troubles—only fellowship with the living God. But how do we get there?

In life, we are placed between two boxcars called heaven and earth. There are times when we want to concentrate on the heavenly, spiritual things. We pray and read Scripture and long for the day when we can be in the presence of the living God. Then there are times when we want to get all the details of this world in order. We plan and then work to control our circumstances, try to achieve some sense of financial and relational stability, and do our best to fit in with society. It is as though we move back and forth between heaven and earth, using our ladders and ropes to try to conquer both.

God created both heaven and earth and laid the two end to end. It would be nice to spend each day in prayer, but how would we pay the bills and care for others? It would be practical to concentrate all our efforts on the concerns of this world, but how would we be connected to God? The answer is to press into both.

When we place a hand and foot in the world and press in, it makes it clear where there is strife, need, and problems that can only be solved by God. When we place a hand and foot in heaven and press in, it makes it clear how the characteristics and tasks connected to the eternal kingdom must be accomplished. It is only when we press into both heaven and earth that we gain the leverage to move to the great and good things that heaven and earth have to offer.

Let us press in on both sides of our spiritual and earthly lives. May we remember the great and good things that God wants to accomplish in us and through us by pressing ourselves "between the boxcars."

Evening Reflection

A Party for You

" 'My son,' the father said, 'you are always with me, and everything I have is yours.' "

LUKE 15:31

Unlike many people who say that life isn't fair (and therefore we should just get on with it), I think God built life to be fair. Fairness is based on justice, which is the essential element in both God's character and his grace. If God is just, then life at its essence should be fair and just.

But caregiving seems to defy the whole idea of what is fair. How is it fair that my child was born with spina bifida? How is it fair that I am the sibling who must care for my elderly mom just because I stayed in the same city to raise my family? How is it fair that my spouse was the one who had the stroke? All these questions seem to scream the same thing: God has somehow forgotten about our faithfulness in giving care. It is not so much that we resent the fact that we are giving loving care, but that everyone else seems to be at the dance and that God doesn't seem to care that we've been left with so much work. On the surface, the caregiver seems to have gotten the short end of the stick from God.

On this issue of fairness, it's always helpful for me to remember the story of the "other son" in the parable of the prodigal. Little brother came to his father and demanded his inheritance so he could eat, drink, and be merry. When the fortunes of little brother turned south, he reasoned to himself that he could go back to his father and be a servant. As he was coming back home, his father saw him and rushed out to greet him. What joy the father felt to have his son return to the fold! But when a servant told the older brother about what was going on, the brother was incredulous.

He went to his father and essentially said, "How dare you! I have been the son who has always been here for you, managing the home place. When things were tough, *I* was the one who was faithful. Through these long years *I* have been the one to love you, but now when little brother returns after squandering our family resources, you give *him* a party. Where is *my* party? Where is the fairness?"

Like the older brother, most caregivers are in situations where we have seen life pass us by. Other families are blessed with good health and seem to move from one glamorous activity to the next. Why not us? We see our siblings carry on normally and even act as though they have no responsibility to care for their own parent. Why not us? We feel left out of normal life, and we are left holding the caregiving bag. And what's worse, often we are not recognized for the sacrifices and efforts we've made. Indeed, where is the fairness?

Thank God that this lifetime is not all there is. You see, God *is* fair and is *very* attentive to our service and effort. As Jesus completes the story of the prodigal, he tells of the father's response to his angry, faithful son: "'My son,' the father said, 'you are always with me, and everything I have is yours'" (Luke 15:31).

Jesus is happy and excited about the lives of brothers, sisters, acquaintances, and friends who never experience the responsibility, obligation, and commitment that caregiving requires. But he is just as happy and excited about your life as a caregiver. He says to us, "You have always been with me," because he himself knows the extreme cost and commitment of caregiving. He says to us, "Everything I have is yours," because he celebrates his treasure and inheritance with us when our race is finished. Does that celebration make up for all the times you and I have missed out on some life experience or had something pass us by? I cannot answer for you, but the answer for me is, "Oh, yes!"

DAY 17

Morning Prayer

May I Be God's Alchemist

*"I will give them an undivided heart and put a new spirit in them;
I will remove from them their heart of stone and give them a heart
of flesh. Then they will follow my decrees and be careful to keep
my laws. They will be my people, and I will be their God."*

Ezekiel 11:19–20

Bill was not a bad man, just a difficult man. When there were
many to serve food to, Bill wanted and *demanded* to be served
first. When he wanted something done, he believed we should
drop whatever we were doing at the time and make his number
one priority our number one priority. He usually emphasized
his requests with demanding anger just to drive the point home
that he wanted immediate attention. And he trusted no one. He
accused his caregivers of stealing, not caring, and trying to take
advantage of him. He wasn't bad, but he was truly difficult.

When I see people such as Bill, I think of the condition of
their hearts. I think about the heart that is resentful because it
isn't as healthy as it once was or wants to be. I think about the
heart that is angry because it must depend on others for something. I think about the heart that is frightened because it thinks
it will be left alone. I think about the heart that is lonely because
others have grown weary of all the resentfulness, anger, and fear
and have simply gone away to find kinder people to deal with.
Bill had this kind of heart; he was an angry, scared, and lonely
man, and what he did each day reflected his heart.

All of us have this kind of heart at times. We know what it's like to feel resentful, angry, scared, and lonely. But we also know there is good in our hearts along with the bad stuff. God is always at work trying to convert that bad stuff into good stuff. God is an alchemist. He can take hearts that are divided and hardened like stone from fear and anger and turn them into living hearts of flesh that are loving and tender. We know that God wants to do this with *our* hearts, and he also wants to do that with hearts like the one Bill has.

I and the other caregivers to Bill decided we would be as loving as we could. When he was demanding, we would say something like, "Bill, I appreciate the fact that you're asking that your need be known to me. I want to respond to you." When he was impatient, we would say something like, "You have a lot of clarity in knowing what you want. Ask, and you will receive." And when he was angry, we would say something like, "Bill, I am here. This is a problem to be solved, and together we can solve it."

Change began to take place, not immediately but gradually. First, Bill became distinctly less demanding. Then his angry outbursts became fewer and fewer. Finally, Bill came to me one day and said, "You know, I've been treated with nothing but kindness and respect here."

I suggested that Bill tell the other caregivers what he had told me, and so he did. His words were usually responded to with a warm hug, which softened Bill even further. Bill was far from perfect, but as his heart became less resentful and fearful, he became gentler and kinder to everyone.

God himself is the alchemist. He alone has the power to transform divided hearts of stone into hearts of living and kind flesh. But I know that having a sickness, injury, or disease that requires caregiving can make the heart sick and fearful. God wants to heal the hearts of those who have this sickness and fear. Today I want to be connected with God's work in turning hearts. I can do so with my encouraging words, loving spirit, and kindness that come from Jesus. May I be God's alchemist in helping to change hearts that are hard to hearts that are soft.

Evening Reflection

The Art of Self-Control

*Apply your heart to instruction
and your ears to words of knowledge.*

PROVERBS 23:12

Listed among the fruit of the Spirit in Galatians is the characteristic of self-control. The idea is a discipline of having control over one's own conduct, emotions, and desires. In a world more than willing to tell us we should say and do what we "feel" because it is somehow unhealthy to keep all these things in, the idea of self-control may sound archaic. But in this discipline, we find the secret to trustworthy and faithful behavior. In short, self-control is about being committed to thinking about the right things and then actually doing the right things. For me, two words describe this discipline: *responsibility* and *reliability*.

Self-control connotes responsibility in terms of acknowledging what our job is. We are assured in Scripture that a battle is going on around us. Satan is creeping about like a lion waiting to devour those who are weak (1 Peter 5:8). We are instructed to gird ourselves to fight all sorts of evil thoughts and behaviors (Ephesians 6:14). God is on our side in this battle and he's given us the Spirit to lead and guide us, but the responsibility of resisting, responding, and realizing evil and good rests with us.

As a caregiver, it is our responsibility to practice self-control over thought patterns such as negativity or depression. It is our responsibility to behave and think in such a way that both we and our care receivers are built up through encouragement and kindness. It is our responsibility to engage in the practice of prayer and the reading of Scripture to fill our minds and hearts with goodness. To effectively practice the art of self-control, we must be committed to the idea of taking the responsibility to put good into our hearts. If we fail, we easily fall victim to the natural bent to become discouraged and disheartened.

But responsibility is only half of the equation. The other half is reliability—the essential quality of building trustworthiness. Reliability displayed when we practice executing our responsibility in a consistent fashion. It is not enough to say we need to set our thoughts on whatever is good, pure, and holy (Philippians 4:8); we must consistently set our thoughts on such attributes.

The same is true as I practice loving care. It is not enough to acknowledge that my caregiving charge is my responsibility; I must consistently execute loving care day after day in order for trustworthiness to be built between two people in a caregiving relationship.

How consistent does our care have to be to be reliable? Think in terms of how consistent you have to be for others to accept a characteristic as part of your personality. For example, if I'm extroverted in my social relationships only half the time and introverted the other half, would my friends call me extroverted? Probably not. Instead they'd say I'm "between" or "confused." In order to have a characteristic attributed to our personality, it must be a part of our character the vast majority of the time—perhaps as much as 90 percent of the time. To be reliable means we are consistent with our responsibility the overwhelming majority of the time.

Self-control lies at the heart of trustworthiness. If we want to practice this discipline, we must concentrate on discovering our responsibility in the spiritual and relational walks of life, and then executing that responsibility in a reliable fashion. God can use such responsibility and reliability in the lives of caregivers to accomplish great things.

DAY 18

Morning Prayer

May I Listen to the Story

The unfolding of your words gives light;
it gives understanding to the simple.
PSALM 119:130

Anne was a fierce woman way beyond her ninety-eight-pound frame. When you would try to get her to do something she didn't want to do—bathe or eat, for example—she'd launch into a tirade of swearwords, often grabbing something to throw at you. Clearly she was used to being in charge and had no intention of relinquishing that position anytime soon.

The problem, of course, was that when she came to the personal care facility where I worked, she needed help desperately. Her hair hadn't been brushed in months and was full of tangles and knots. Her teeth were in terrible shape and needed care badly. Her clothes were soiled, and, quite frankly, she stunk from not bathing for a very long time. Her memory was bad, her nutrition was in dire straits, and more and more things were physically beginning to malfunction. But short of wrestling her down, I was at a loss as to how to get her the help she needed.

I tried speaking with her in a calm and reassuring voice. "Don't patronize me," she fired back. I tried speaking in a firm and responsible voice. "You think you're tougher than me? I'll show you tough," she snarled as she hurled a hairbrush at me. Reasoning with her just wasn't going to work. I saw little alternative except to have her leave the facility.

97

As I talked with my wife about Anne one evening, Sharon asked me about some of Anne's circumstances. "What did she do during her working years? What was her husband's name and what did he do? How did she cope before she came here?" A bit embarrassed, I realized I knew none of the answers to these questions. I had simply been telling Anne what she needed and what I needed her to do. I hadn't taken the time to find out anything about her.

I really didn't think anything would make a difference, but I went to see Anne the next morning. "What do you want!" she barked.

"I'd like to find out a bit more about you," I said.

Anne gave me a long, hard look and said softly, "What do you want to know?"

I asked her about her life in the city where we lived, about her husband and son, about her work, and about some of her thoughts and struggles. In the course of forty-five minutes, she had given me a wealth of information about her life.

As it turned out, Anne was a working woman when not many women worked outside the home. She eventually managed a significant number of people at the telephone company. When her husband retired and had a heart attack, she was totally responsible for his care for the last two years of his life. This was a woman who knew how to get things done. She was a woman of resiliency and courage who had faced hard times and come through strong and confident.

I went back to my office realizing I had only thought of Anne in terms of what I wanted her to do. I hadn't taken into account her past capabilities, her way of thinking, and her preferences. I had forgotten that she had a whole different life apart from her need.

I went back to Anne's apartment in the afternoon and said, "Anne, I apologize. After our conversation this morning, I realized how strong and confident you are and how I offended you by telling you what needed to be done. I will simply tell you what I see, and you can tell me what needs to be done."

Anne stared at me again, and I expected to get another hairbrush thrown at me. Instead, she asked me what I saw. I started with her hair, and she told me how to remove knots. I followed her instructions meticulously and for the first time in months, her hair was combed. By the end of the week, following Anne's instructions, she was clean, eating, and doing much better.

A person's story, no matter how long or short, is really where the essence of their personality and history is located. It is almost impossible to understand someone apart from their story. When we take the time to learn about the ones we care for and who and what they are—or in some cases remind ourselves who and what they are—we open a door to understand, relate, and cooperate. When we bark orders, we offend and often suspend our relationships.

In my effort to give care, I always want to be a person who seeks to hear where people are coming from, and that means I must hear their story. May I be committed, this day, to listen and understand the story that defines the person to whom I give care.

Evening Reflection

The Power of Narrative

"This is why I speak to them in parables:

'Though seeing, they do not see;
though hearing, they do not hear or
understand.'"

MATTHEW 13:13

In our sound-bite world, we know words are powerful things. One slip-up with an inappropriate phrase or saying the wrong word can mean the end to a politician's aspirations or a superstar's career. But what is lost in the sound bite of our fast-moving, media-oriented society is the fact that story, or narrative, is much more powerful. The words of one day are only a snapshot of what a person was wearing for one hour of life. Narrative contains the history of a person's closet of all they have owned and worn, as well as which outfits are well liked and which are most scorned.

Narrative is important for many reasons in our lives. First, in the story of a person we find the enduring characteristics that reveal personality and values. When I think about any one particular day of my wife's caregiving for my mother-in-law, Genevieve, it may look somewhat unspectacular. But if I think about the entire process of caregiving, it reveals how my wife was loyal, faithful to the task, and sacrificial in her giving.

Second, the narrative of a person's life tells us about the wisdom of lessons learned. I recall one woman's recounting of the terrible loss her family suffered in a car accident and her subsequent struggle at rehabilitation. "I learned something very important from all of this," she said. "I've learned that even though you never know where God is going to take you in life, you must keep trying to be faithful, because he is faithful to you."

Third, in the course of narrative, you discover the flow of purpose that God intends. Scripture is not just a collection of stories; it is a story, a narrative, in itself. The whole of Scripture tells us that God is involved with us and loves us and that he is committed to redeeming our relationship with him totally and completely.

Narrative does so much for us. It tells of a person's value or character; it tells us of wisdom gained and lessons learned; it tells us of the meaning and purpose of life. In short, narrative gives us the chance to pull out meaning and purpose. It is a wonderful gift from God and one he uses with us in teaching. Jesus' main method of teaching was not preaching but the telling of stories (see Mark 4:2).

As a caregiver, you are engaged in a great narrative. In the day-to-day events of cleaning, cooking, dispensing medications, helping with bathroom needs, dressing, and connecting, you are constructing a story. The only question is what this narrative will say about your meaning and purpose. Will the story of your caregiving reveal patient and loving service, wisdom from lessons learned, and spiritual truths that are timeless? Or will your story reveal just one monotonous day after another that points to nowhere?

I have no doubt that God uses the story of caregiving to shape a caregiver's character, values, and spiritual direction. In many ways, caregiving and its challenges are God's way of speaking to us. But our eyes and ears need to be open so we can discern what he is trying to say.

The narrative is all around us and is still being written. Let us not just experience the story; let us live the story to the fullest and tell the narrative of how God has used occurrences to shape in us lessons, values, and spiritual truths.

DAY 19

Morning Prayer

May I Catch a Glimpse of the Church Triumphant

So will it be with the resurrection of the dead. The body that is sown is perishable, it is raised imperishable; it is sown in dishonor, it is raised in glory; it is sown in weakness, it is raised in power; it is sown a natural body, it is raised a spiritual body.

1 CORINTHIANS 15:42–44

"When am I going to get better?" It is a hard question with no easy answer for terminal patients and their caregivers.

Sadie was a woman who seemed to have so much to live for. She enjoyed spending time with her four young grandchildren, traveling with her husband, and working at a job where she was well respected. But now after surgery for cancer, the news wasn't good. The cancer had spread to her lymph nodes, and there were signs that its voracious appetite would not be stopped until it had run its course.

"When am I going to get better?" she groggily asked her husband, who had been a hero of a caregiver for the last thirteen months as Sadie went from treatment to treatment.

I waited to hear his answer, thinking there was no way he'd be able to answer the question well and truthfully. He proved me wrong.

"Well, girlfriend," he said, choking his tears back, "just a little while longer on this side, and then you will be absolutely perfect and well on the other."

Sadie stared at her husband for a couple of minutes, then breathed a heavy sigh. Peacefully, she looked at him and said, "Well, that is good news."

Good news indeed! There is no such thing as caregiving for someone who has no need and is in perfect condition. Caregiving goes hand in hand with need, sickness, injury, deterioration, malady, and imperfections. Sometimes the people we care for do get better, but for most of us caregivers, we'll witness the long roller-coaster ride of rally and decline that eventually slows to a downward spiral or a progressive march to deterioration and death. It is not easy, but for those who are believers, there is this good news: we will someday have a new body that will be imperishable, glorious, and powerful.

When Jesus arrived at the home of his friend Lazarus, he was informed that he was too late and that Lazarus had been dead for days and was laid to final rest in the tomb. But Jesus raised Lazarus from the dead. This miracle, however, was not a *resurrection*; it was a *resuscitation*. In other words, Jesus restored Lazarus to a living state — but one Lazarus had already been in before he died.

Resurrection is something totally different. Our bodies and the bodies of the people we care for are fragile, perishable, weak — not built for the spiritual world. When believers die, there is an actual remaking of the body, similar to the kind of body Jesus had when he was raised from the dead. This body cannot break and become sick. This body cannot decay or perish but will last forever. In short, this new body is built for a spiritual purpose fit for God's eternal kingdom. When are we going to get better? We will be totally healed and made right when we receive our resurrected body.

The person we care for is not locked into the downward spiral of decay forever. He or she will not have to suffer with the indignations of disease and sickness for eternity. The day will come when he or she is presented with a wholesome spiritual body that doesn't require care from anyone. These eternal bodies are the promise of the church triumphant. All who believe will have this type of glorious body in which to sing and offer praises to God throughout eternity.

So when we look at the person to whom we give care, let us always remember that the problems we address are only temporary. He or she, and all of us who believe, will one day be completely healed and made completely whole.

May we always remember that our caregiving is temporary because we belong to the church triumphant.

Evening Reflection

Bearing the Cross for Jesus

I have been crucified with Christ and I no longer live, but Christ lives in me. The life I live in the body, I live by faith in the Son of God, who loved me and gave himself for me.

GALATIANS 2:20

"Who, me?" "Yes, you." With that improbable exchange, Simon from Cyrene was pressed into service, carrying the cross for Jesus as Jesus walked the road to his crucifixion.

I've often wondered what Simon felt when he was selected to carry out this task. I can imagine him thinking, "All I was doing was minding my own business, and now I'm caught up with this thing that has nothing to do with me." Or maybe, "Just play it cool and get the job done, and they'll leave you alone." Surely Simon was just an innocent bystander involved in his normal course of life and never expected to be pressed into service on the Savior's behalf.

But just as striking is to think about Simon in the subsequent days, when he surely learned that this Jesus was really somebody special and different. Perhaps Simon eventually came to believe in Jesus. What would Simon have done with the reality of his act, knowing that he brushed up against God in the climax of the history of redemption? Perhaps he thought, "I was there to help bear the load of the cross when the Savior would bear alone the load of my sin and the sin of the world."

In a way, caregivers are pressed into similar service. I doubt that any of us had on our five-year "goals and objectives" plan to become a caregiver of a loved one. But just as he said to Simon, God said to us, "Yes, you," when the child was born with serious problems or someone in our family got sick or old. Certainly Jesus, were he here in flesh and blood, would have a heart for those who need care. It would be his desire and passion to heal and to give care. The person in need of care would be the burden that Jesus would gladly bear on his way to redeeming all of us. But Jesus isn't here in flesh and blood—except through our flesh and blood. The difference between us and Simon is that we definitely know who the Savior is when we are called to bear part of his load. So what do we do with such a reality?

Caregiving isn't just a string of tasks we do until we are let off the hook by death or by relief from another caregiver. It is a job that has deep spiritual meaning in that we are called to be colaborers or co-cross bearers with Jesus. Paul recognized this truth when he declared, "I have been crucified with Christ and I no longer live, but Christ lives in me. The life I live in the body, I live by faith in the Son of God, who loved me and gave himself for me" (Galatians 2:20).

As caregivers, our names have been called and we've been pressed into service. We can choose to grumble about our "bad luck," or we can simply serve our time until we are released. But in reality, we have the opportunity to connect with the very heart and purpose of Jesus. Let us seize this opportunity to know his heart and work and bind ourselves totally to his purpose.

DAY 20

Morning Prayer

May I Feel the Wound

*He himself bore our sins in his body on the tree,
so that we might die to sins and live for righteousness;
by his wounds you have been healed.*

1 PETER 2:24

I must admit I find little good in the process of demential. The gift of medical science that has brought us longer life unfortunately cannot guarantee that we will stay healthy or high functioning. The fact is, the longer we live, especially into our eighties, the greater the chance we will develop Alzheimer's disease or some type of dementia. And make no mistake, dementia brings a tremendous amount of pain. From the perspective of the person with the disease, he or she is forced to watch in horror as personality and identity increasingly slip away. From the perspective of the caregiver, we must deal with development in reverse, as the retrograde of reasoning robs the person of even basic problem solving and makes it impossible to carry out even the most elemental life functions.

I ask a question of almost everyone I meet who cares for a person with severe dementia or Alzheimer's: "How do you continue to function, knowing that things will only get worse?" Most say they simply take one day at a time, which is, of course, a great and resilient answer.

But one day a caregiver named Louise gave me the best answer I've ever heard: "I have to remember that all of us are imperfect and carry wounds. Just because I'm currently less wounded or more capable than the one I care for does not mean that I don't have wounds. Yet Christ was more than willing to bear my wounds for me and redeem them so they will be eventually perfect. It is a privilege for me, then, to bear someone else's wounds. I can't make the wounds go away, but I can do my part in redeeming the wound—trying to lessen its impact. It's a job I share with Christ."

What a testimony to Christ's work in us. We are all imperfect and flawed. Christ is willing to take on those imperfections and flaws for the purpose of redemption. But we need to be realistic in that when Christ takes on these imperfections and flaws, it costs him a very real price and results in pain.

Remember when the bleeding woman sought to touch Jesus because she believed that if she could only touch him, she would be healed? When she pressed through the crowd and successfully made contact with his garment, Jesus observed, "Someone touched me; I know that power has gone out from me" (Luke 8:46). The power that left Jesus went to the woman's wound to give her healing.

Louise knew this kind of power. She knew the power that left the Savior and went into her to heal her wounds, and she also knew the power that left her in order to compensate for the wounds of the one to whom she gave care.

When we as caregivers touch pain, wounds, and malfunctions, we are working with Christ to ameliorate what is wrong in the world. It is one of the great and real things that God has given us the privilege of doing as we serve as colaborers in his kingdom.

But we must also be realistic. When we touch those wounds, seek to heal pain, or compensate for a person's lack of ability to function, some of that wound goes to us. We feel the pain, and we don't function as well. Just as Christ takes on our wounds as his, so we take on others' wounds as ours. It costs us something, but it also joins us to the heart of Christ. His work is our work.

Today, let us seek to feel the wounds and pain of our loved one and compensate and heal that wound through the power of Christ.

Evening Reflection

Giving Over Our Power Voluntarily

What, then, shall we say in response to this?
If God is for us, who can be against us?

ROMANS 8:31

Perhaps nothing is as hard as giving up power that brings recognition. The story is told of Cincinnatus, a Roman hero who at the request of leaders took control of the empire to defeat an ominous threat. After the victory, Cincinnatus could have had complete control of the empire and ruled as an infallible dictator. Instead, after the threat was removed, he resigned his power voluntarily and went back to the life of farming to provide for his family. At the height of his power, he chose to be humble and not misuse the power that was available. His story has stood for the ages as an example of how to be a true leader and public servant.

Peter, on the other hand, was no Cincinnatus. Peter was a guy with a devout passion for the mission of Christ. When Peter was called, he immediately followed Jesus (Matthew 4:19–20). When Jesus walked on water, Peter wanted in (Matthew 14:28). When it came to understanding who Jesus was, Peter stated clearly that Jesus was the Christ (Matthew 16:16).

But Peter also had clear ideas about how to make the mission of Christ come about. When Jesus started talking about his eventual death and resurrection, Peter would have none of it and told Jesus he wouldn't let it happen (Matthew 16:22). When Jesus tried to give a lesson in servanthood by washing the disciples' feet, Peter initially scorned it (John 13:8). As Jesus was taken into custody, Peter drew his sword to protect the Savior (John 18:10). Each time, Peter was rebuked harshly by Jesus. Peter must have wondered, "How do I help this guy? I try to do what I think is best—and it's all rejected. How can I be so far off?"

Of course, the story of Peter culminates with his rejection and denial of Jesus. Peter must have concluded that he was totally disloyal, uncommitted, and useless to the cause of Christ. He must have thought that his life of ministry was over and that there was nothing left to do but go back to fishing—which was, apparently, where Jesus intended to lead Peter to all along. When the resurrected Jesus confronts Peter on the lake, he asks him if he loves him. When Peter answers in the affirmative, Jesus responds, "Feed my sheep" (John 21:17). After the third question, Jesus foretells the way in which Peter will die and commands him to "follow me!"

Peter follows, a broken man—a man with no power to resist Jesus. A man with no idea of how to accomplish the ministry on his own. A man whose character had been erased so he could experience the character and strength of Jesus. A man who would eventually come to know God's way so well that he wouldn't be afraid to stand up to any civil authority and would be willing to suffer any indignation or suffering and be crucified upside down rather than to disown Jesus again. Peter was a man who, when he finally gave up power over his own life, would find the life Jesus intended him to have all along.

Jesus has a particular aspect of character picked out that he wants to develop in you. He wanted Peter to become dependent on God's way instead of his own and to have the unwavering conviction of God's strength. What has God picked out for you? Learning to be patient? To be giving? Is it to develop joy or kindness? God and you are the only ones who know the answer, but to get this work accomplished, you must be willing to give your personality and character to God. You must resign the power if God is to develop in you what he wants. You may follow the example of Cincinnatus and give the power over to God voluntarily. You may choose to follow Peter's example and hang on to your power the best way you can. Either way, God will eventually develop the aspect of character he has for you.

DAY 21

Morning Prayer

May I Be a Worthy Teacher of Caregiving

*Therefore this is what the LORD, who redeemed Abraham,
    says to the house of Jacob:*

"*No longer will Jacob be ashamed;
    no longer will their faces grow pale.
When they see among them their children,
    the work of my hands,
they will keep my name holy;
    they will acknowledge the holiness of the
        Holy One of Jacob,
    and will stand in awe of the God of Israel.*"

ISAIAH 29:22–23

I have a friend with a particularly impatient nature when he gets behind the wheel of his car. He seldom, if ever, edits his thoughts about how other people are driving. He consistently yells at, comments on, or degrades the driver who makes an improper signal, who isn't going fast enough to suit him, or who changes lanes at a time inconvenient to him. We often laughed at his stories of the crazy things people do when they drive and his overzealous reactions, considering both of them things that would never change.

But one day my friend said, "I'm through with my comments about the way other people drive."

I thought skeptically, "Sure you are—until tomorrow when that driver cuts you off."

But then he told me the reason for his newfound commitment to patience and kindness on the road. Earlier in the day he was driving his three-year-old son to day care. When he pulled up behind a woman at a stop sign, the three-year-old yelled from the backseat, "Out of the way, you old bag!"

"Where did you learn that?" my friend said to his son, confident he had always edited his language when the kids were in the car.

"From you, Daddy," his son said. "I want to help you get me to school on time."

It's a lesson most of us learn the hard way. Our children do not do as we say as much as they do as we do. Everything we do in the way of living, being, and behaving is being watched by the coming generation, and our actions have a huge impact on the way our children think, feel, and eventually act.

Take a few minutes to think about yourself. Do you carry the same political party affiliation as your parents? Do you have the same or a better standard of living than your parents? Do you carry at least a few of the same bigotries or beliefs as your parents have with regard to other ethnicities or groups? Chances are if you're like most people, you answered yes to at least one of the questions. What makes us think we carry any less influence with our children?

There are currently some forty million caregivers in the United States. And most of us, in one way or another, will eventually give care to another human being—maybe for a child or a spouse who is disabled, a neighbor who has no one else to look out for him or her, or an elderly parent who is increasingly becoming dependent. We have, or may soon have, the task of caregiving, and there is a generation of future caregivers in our children who will be watching us.

Do we complain and grumble about having to be a caregiver? Do we belittle the people we care for and speak negatively about them because we think they are somehow "less" than us? Do we make fun of the lack of abilities of the ones in our charge? If so, remember that someone in the backseat of our caregiving car is watching and learning from our every move in this area. Curses and sins aren't passed along to our children only in terms of our financial legacies or reputations; they are also passed along in terms of our attitudes, prejudices, and bad habits. As Lamentations 5:7 reminds us, "Our fathers sinned and are no more, and we bear their punishment."

But here is the good news: our children also learn from our patience, love, joy, and peace. When we give of ourselves in unselfish and positive ways, they also have the opportunity to see that caregiving is a wonderful gift for both the one being cared for and the one doing the caring. Our children learn that love and care for those in need is a service not only to the person in need but also to the God who loves humility and kindness.

When we honor God through our lives and caregiving, our children learn to do the same. They learn to stand in awe of God. May they learn from us as worthy teachers of caregiving.

Evening Reflection

You Are Beloved

How great is the love the Father has lavished on us, that we should be called children of God! And that is what we are!

1 JOHN 3:1

Although I didn't know him well or for very long before his death, I had two occasions to speak with well-known author and priest Henri Nouwen. One of the things Henri never tired of talking about was God's love. I remember how vibrantly he spoke of the Holy Spirit's descending on Jesus just after baptism, and the Father's words: "You are my Son, whom I love; with you I am well pleased" (Luke 3:22).

God's words were not a pep talk about Jesus' earthly ministry. They were not a command about where to go next. Henri would say, "It was an affirmation of how totally and completely Jesus was loved by the Father." In other words, nothing was closer to the heart of God than making sure that his Son knew how completely loved he was and that his being was totally endearing to the Father.

Most of us have people in our lives who make us feel loved because of the sacrifices they make for us, the gifts they give us, or the words of encouragement they speak. But only a few are genuinely excited about us as people. I hope you know what I'm talking about.

One such person was "Aunt" Wanda, a two-hundred-pound, five-foot-tall woman with a passion for people. She greeted me loudly and heartily, always making physical contact. She looked into my eyes deeply, but playfully. Her eyes beamed and brought a smile to the depths of my soul. She was enthusiastic about every story I told and engaged in every aspect of my being. And when she left, I really, really felt loved. I always felt as though she had given a shot of life directly into my vein, and I wanted to roll up my sleeve to get one in the other arm.

This is the picture of what God is communicating when he says, "This is my Son, whom I love; with him I am well pleased" (Matthew 3:17). Here we see not a stately or reserved God but a Father who is consumed and overwhelmed by the love he has for Jesus.

This is also the love that God has for you. The truth is, God is completely taken with you as his creation. He takes great joy in the way you walk and talk. He sees the very best in what you will become and is thrilled to be with you. He has no shame about you, but only light and life that he wants to inject into your heart and veins. He loves the daylights out of you.

As caregivers, we have so many tasks to perform. It helps to remember that we bear the cross with Jesus and that we are cola-borers in the process of ministry with him. It is good for us to know that the work we do has eternal consequences and plays a role in mediating pain and suffering. But it is most important of all to remember that we are not loved by God as caregivers first; we are, above all, loved by God because we are people who are distinctly *his people*.

We hear plenty of voices in our heads that say things like, "You are ugly, worthless, and undesirable." We need to hear the resounding voice of God confirming to us that we are his beloved sons and daughters. We are completely beautiful to him. We are his prized possessions and the apple of his eye. He sees nothing but our ultimate and perfected potential, and he desires nothing more than to be with us.

Sometimes we need to remember how loved we really are and how pleased God is with our personhood. So roll up your sleeve and get an injection of God's love as he proclaims, "You are my beloved child!"

DAY 22

Morning Prayer

May I Connect to People, Not Stuff

*"Do not store up for yourselves treasures on earth, where
moth and rust destroy, and where thieves break in and steal.
But store up for yourselves treasures in heaven, where moth and
rust do not destroy, and where thieves do not break in and steal.
For where your treasure is, there your heart will be also."*

MATTHEW 6:19–21

For a time I served as a director of a personal care facility. We met the basic caregiving needs of folks who had to have help but didn't have medical conditions requiring full-time nursing. Not only did I serve as the director, but my wife and I also lived on the property and observed as resident after resident came and went.

As sad as a "move out" was, signaling that a person had died or now needed a higher level of care, sadder still was a "move in." It was on these days that a resident and his or her family would take all the stuff that had accumulated for years and try to cram it into a small, one-room efficiency apartment. Of course, the precious belongings that took years of sacrifice and work to purchase just wouldn't fit. To the horror of the resident, the realization dawned that most of the "stuff" he or she worked so hard for was going to be stored, given away, or thrown away. It was an important life lesson for my wife and me: the things we had purchased for our home would one day be considered just "stuff."

But one spirited, lovely woman named Alice was the perfect contrast. She came to the apartment with a small bed, one dresser, and a couple of chairs. From the moment she hit the facility, she made it her goal to learn everyone's name. Every time someone walked into her room to give her medication, change her sheets, help her do a chore, or help her dress, she asked questions about the caregiver or tried to give away a piece of candy. Alice always seemed 100 percent behind the idea that it was important to make others feel better while they cared for her.

I admired Alice for several reasons, and I wanted to find out her secret for living life wisely. "I always make it a point to connect with people," she said. "The way I have it figured out, what people think about you is the only real thing that you'll leave behind."

"Is that why you hardly have any stuff?" I asked.

"Honey," she said, "stuff just has to be taken care of and won't do one thing for you in the end. I've learned that when you take care of people, they'll take care of you back."

Indeed, each personal care aide in my building, including me, loved to take care of Alice because she always made sure to take care of us in some way.

Most caregivers are of quite modest means. We usually don't think of investing in fancy furniture or clothes, and many of us have trouble making financial ends meet. But that doesn't mean we've learned the lesson of Alice. You see, "stuff" is whatever takes us away from our focus on loving God more or loving fellow human beings as ourselves.

For caregivers, stuff is likely to be the overemphasis we give to maintaining physical health for the one we care for, or perhaps being overly zealous about the schedule and a particular medication regimen. The truth is, just as "stuff" we buy—furniture, clothes, and so on—will wear out, get scratched, and eventually become junk, so will the physical health of our loved one and the obsolete schedule we worked so hard to maintain.

Remember the parable Jesus told of a prosperous man who had a great harvest. This man told himself, "This is what I'll do. I will tear down my barns and build bigger ones, and there I will store all my grain and my goods" (Luke 12:18). All his work accomplished, this man then said to himself, "You have plenty of good things laid up for many years. Take life easy; eat, drink and be merry" (verse 19).

But then God spoke up. And this is what he said to the man: "You fool! This very night your life will be demanded from you. Then who will get what you have prepared for yourself?" (verse 20).

May we be like Alice, who knew the value of making an eternal investment in people and who refused to give her life to the accumulation of "stuff."

Evening Reflection

The Advantage of Being a Care Receiver

> *"Blessed are the poor in spirit,*
> *for theirs is the kingdom of heaven."*
>
> MATTHEW 5:3

Lawrence was a schizophrenic with significant problems. He was always on the move from one place to the next, trying to stabilize his life, going to the doctor to get treatment for arthritis, trying to find his next meal. But every time the church doors were open for prayer and worship, Lawrence was there. Sure, he was there partly because people looked out for him and helped him out. But there were many times when no one would give him anything—and Lawrence was just as happy and satisfied praising God and the goodness of being alive. Lawrence seemed to have nothing and at the same time seemed to have everything.

Jesus spent much of his time with the poor and preaching good news to them, as was foretold in Scripture (see Isaiah 61:1). The poor have nothing—nothing to hold on to, nothing to control, nothing with which to brace themselves from the elements of life, nothing to lose. This is what makes the hearts of the poor such fertile ground for the gospel of Jesus. They are not threatened with the possibility of giving something up—wealth or lifestyle, for example—and there is nothing they can use to hide their extreme vulnerability and need.

Very simply, the poor experience all the rejection, harshness, and trauma the world has to offer, and they have nothing with which to protect themselves. So when it comes to the gospel, they have nothing to lose from accepting grace, for their hope truly lies in the life to come.

Jesus pounded this truth home after he encountered a rich young man who loved his possessions: "I tell you the truth, it is hard for a rich man to enter the kingdom of heaven. Again I tell you, it is easier for a camel to go through the eye of a needle than for a rich man to enter the kingdom of God" (Matthew 19:23–24). It is hard for a rich man because he has so much, but it's easier for a poor man because he has so little.

Care receivers also have something of this same advantage. Most of us think that the people who need care are cursed by their sickness or maladies. They have little to protect themselves from dependence on others and are very limited in their ability to physically exert power or to control their own lives. In many ways, they are naked because they have very little ability to hide infirmities because of the fact that they receive care.

But where most of us see a tragedy or shortcoming, God actually sees advantage. It is easier for those who have little, for those who are in need, to accept the promise and life that God has to offer. Who would not accept God's offer to have a resurrected body if you could not walk or experienced pain with every step you took?

But it's important to remember the words of Jesus—"it is easier for a camel to go through the eye of a needle." This is true for a rich man trying to get to the vulnerable point of being poor in spirit, and it's also true for a strong and healthy caregiver trying to get to the vulnerable point of being needy and unable to care for one's self. The truth about life is that none of us—rich or poor, strong or weak—can manage life or can enter eternity without God. We all do better when we come to this realization and give ourselves over to God, asking him to manage our lives because we have no hope of managing our lives ourselves.

As caregivers, we need to seek the kind of humble, vulnerable, and naked spirit that exists with care receivers. Spiritually and emotionally, we all are in the same condition—we need God desperately!

DAY 23

Morning Prayer

May I Remember That I Am More Than a Caregiver

*"I will follow you, Lord; but first let me go
back and say good-by to my family."
Jesus replied, "No one who puts his hand to the plow
and looks back is fit for service in the kingdom of God."*
LUKE 9:61–62

All caregivers know the stress of being pulled in multiple directions at one time. Our caregiving charge has a doctor appointment while across town our child is giving a recital. We need to be fixing a meal for our loved ones and instead we're in the emergency room with the person who needs care.

Because the job of caregiving is so intense and constant, we sometimes begin to think of ourselves as only a caregiver and feel guilty when we do anything else. But many of us are employees, earning an income on which our family depends and performing tasks needed by our employers. Many of us are parents and grandparents who have children or grandchildren needing our attention, nurture, and time. Many of us are married and have friends needing our affection, support, and companionship.

We have many different roles and titles besides that of caregiver, and these obligations are no less pressing. How do we balance these obligations? Although the answer may not be satisfying, it seems fairly clear: we cannot balance the obligations because there are just too many things that require our time and attention—especially when we are a caregiver.

Remember when Jesus was faced with would-be disciples who requested time from him before they agreed to follow him? He invited one man to come along, but the man replied, "Lord, first let me go and bury my father." Jesus responded, "Let the dead bury their own dead, but you go and proclaim the kingdom of God" (Luke 9:59–60).

Was Jesus just being difficult and unsympathetic? I don't think so. I believe Jesus was declaring to the man the reality about life—that there would be no better time to do what God was calling us to do and we need to be responsive when we are called. Simply stated, balancing everything in life is a worthy goal but an illusion. It is much better to recognize what needs to be done next and do it without looking back.

With so many needs and demands, it is often difficult to determine which need is most pressing. In general, I believe most caregivers spend the vast percentage of their time on care-giving tasks. Other family members and friends often pay the price and are poorer because of our absence.

Caregiving is intense, but we do need to fulfill other roles and obligations, not only for the sakes of others but also for our own. It is part of what it means to take care of ourselves and also part of what it means to take care of God's charge to us as expressed in the other obligations he has given us.

As you care for your other obligations, what will happen to the person you give care to? Certainly I'm not advocating neglect, but I am advocating that you explore home health care alternatives or respite care so you can be more of the complete person God intended you to be. You can and should do this without being consumed by worry or guilt about what will happen to the person you care for. If something happens while you are away or the care isn't given exactly as you would do it, you must real-ize that God doesn't give you the luxury of only concentrating on one aspect of your life and that you are not an omnipotent caregiver. God can handle things while you are carrying out the other responsibilities he has for you.

When I was in college, I had a friend who performed the "spinning plates on poles" trick. He would first get one spinning; soon there'd be five and then eight and so on. Amazed at his ability, I once asked for his secret. "Keep moving," he said with a grin. As I started to laugh, he added, "And know when to take the plates down."

You need to know when to take down your caregiving plate so you'll be able to keep up with all the other responsibilities and people who need you. May we always be aware that we are more than caregivers and that we have other roles and responsibilities to carry out as well.

Evening Reflection

Living Life Well

I know what it is to be in need, and I know what it is to have plenty. I have learned the secret of being content in any and every situation, whether well fed or hungry, whether living in plenty or in want. I can do everything through him who gives me strength.

PHILIPPIANS 4:12–13

When we think of living life well, we often think of coming to the end of the race and reflecting back on what has been accomplished and on what people will say about the meaning of our lives. In my own life, I think of wanting others to remember how I influenced many and tried to live in a humble manner. I think about my hope that my loved ones will inscribe on my tombstone the words I've adopted as my life goal: he was a doer of the word and not merely a hearer (see James 1:22). If this can be said about me, I will have lived life well.

The trouble with such a time frame is that it is based on our recollections and memories. We do not stumble through life hoping for the best and then one day reach the end and draw lofty conclusions about the final evaluation of our years. Rather, the measure of living life well occurs in how we handle the specific hours and days of life.

Like many, I have struggled with a clinical depression that has hounded me from time to time. One of my friends told me, "Your depression may last the rest of your life. It came when you didn't want it to come, and there is no promise that it will end. If the depression lasts the rest of your life, you must learn how to live your depression well." The secret to living life well is not to think in terms of the whole or the end of life but to think of how we can live each circumstance of our lives well.

Job lived through what is arguably the worst of circumstances. He was in deep depression and grief. At one point he moaned, "My eyes have grown dim with grief; my whole frame is but a shadow" (Job 17:7). Job's friends thought he was doing something wrong and encouraged him to clean up his act. But Job knew that sin was not the issue. His wife believed that God had cursed Job; Job should in turn curse God. But Job knew that God was faithful. Job endured the pain served up to him, not really knowing the purpose or reason, and lived life faithfully. He lived his depression well.

Paul also had a variety of life circumstances that pressed him at every turn. He experienced warmth and prestige, support and persecution, success and failure throughout the years of his ministry. He came to this firm conclusion: "I know what it is to be in need, and I know what it is to have plenty. I have learned the secret of being content in any and every situation, whether well fed or hungry, whether living in plenty or in want. I can do everything through him who gives me strength" (Philippians 4:12–13). Paul knew the secret isn't in accomplishing big things or balancing hard times with good times. The secret is in faithfulness to God and the determination to live the circumstance well.

Caregiving presents no less of a challenge than depression, grief, or persecution. Most of the time, caregiving has a little of these characteristics each day. The measure of whether we live our caregiving lives well is not in the health or welfare of our charge but in how faithful we are in the task of serving. Is our focus in our caregiving, hour by hour, to love and to be open to love? Do we encourage the person we care for, even when circumstances are discouraging? Do we trust that God is active and knows what he's doing, even when everything seems to be falling apart?

These, I am convinced, are the elements that determine whether we live our caregiving lives well. It is our faithfulness to know that God is at work, that we can be positive in the face of discouragement and loving in our servanthood. If we live this faithfulness hour by hour, then days turn into months and months into years, and we will finally hear the "well done, good and faithful servant." Faithfulness is built by leaning on the strength of the Holy Spirit and the assurance that Christ is for us and active in our lives. Let us learn to live life well by learning to depend on God in each and every circumstance.

DAY 24

Morning Prayer

May I Resolve Broken Relationships

"If you are offering your gift at the altar and there remember that your brother has something against you, leave your gift there in front of the altar. First go and be reconciled to your brother; then come and offer your gift."

MATTHEW 5:23–24

One of the great opportunities I've had is to travel in Europe with my family. My wife and I have an adventuresome spirit, so we almost always drive to the places we want to see after we arrive at the airport.

On one trip, we entered the lovely Italian city of Verona—the setting for Shakespeare's *Romeo and Juliet*. We were trying to find our way to the piazza, with only a vague map in hand and no knowledge of the Italian language. We spotted the lovely square, but somehow in my effort to find a parking place, I took a wrong turn and ended up on the piazza itself.

I couldn't turn back on the one-way street, so there was only one thing left to do. I crept over the rough cobblestones, which were strictly closed to car traffic. Hundreds, perhaps thousands, of people were aghast at my stupid move, yelling at me and shaking their heads and fists. Our children in the backseat had slunk below the window to protect themselves from the gawking crowd and the ridicule of their father's mistake. I had no choice but to apologetically acknowledge my error and keep moving. My only consolation was that it was highly unlikely I would ever have any experience with the people of Verona again.

Family relationships are often difficult. Sometimes we have broken relationships with a father, mother, brother, or sister, only to be thrown into a future situation where we have to give that person care or cooperate with that person to provide necessary care for someone. Maybe the arguments, bad blood, or difficulties happened decades ago, but like my trip to Verona, we still carry the vivid memories of emotional embarrassment or transgressions in our hearts. When faced with dealing with these unresolved situations, we wish we could slink into the backseat, where no one can see us.

The prophet Jonah knew something about this. He had received an important message from God: "Go to the great city of Nineveh and preach against it, because its wickedness has come up before me" (Jonah 1:2). Jonah knew exactly where he was supposed to go, but he was afraid the people of Nineveh would kill him for such a message. So he ended up taking the wrong path. He ran away from God and got on a boat to the wrong city. He was thrown overboard and swallowed by a big fish.

After Jonah came to his senses and prayed for deliverance, the fish spit him up on the shore. There God repeated the message: "Go to the great city of Nineveh and proclaim to it the message I give you" (3:2). In other words, God declared to Jonah, "You got off track when you didn't follow my command. To get back on track, you must obey the same command." Jonah did eventually go to Nineveh and preach, and Nineveh repented and was saved.

Who knows the twists and turns of life? God does. And God knows that even after decades of broken relationships, even in those instances where we don't remember what the conflict was about, we have an opportunity to set things right. Caregiving, among other things, can heal relationships because there is a task that must be done. As a result, it carries with it the opportunity to set right old relationships, old emotional wounds, and old unresolved issues. But to set things right, we must be willing to return to the time and place where things went wrong.

Jonah left God's way when he refused to go to Nineveh. When did you leave God's way? Was it when a family member mistreated you? When you had harsh words with a person? When you resolved in your heart that you would never be open to this person again? Whatever the situation and no matter how much time has elapsed, the caregiving responsibility has opened the way to get back on the path of doing right. Perhaps it comes through an apology, a kind word, or an honest discussion about the past. But whatever it entails, use the opportunity to get back on the path of going God's way.

I may never return to Verona, but eventually I will have to return to my broken family relationships. May we always be open to the resolution of relationships that are brought back to us because of the necessity of caregiving.

 *Evening Reflection*

The Rhythm of Rightness

Let us not become weary in doing good, for at the proper time we will reap a harvest if we do not give up. Therefore, as we have opportunity, let us do good to all people, especially to those who belong to the family of believers.

GALATIANS 6:9–10

I hold to the belief that other things in your life require attention besides caregiving—roles, relationships, and activities that you have an obligation to maintain. But it is undeniable that caregiving demands a significant part of you and requires sacrifice—a sacrifice that will sometimes penetrate to the very root of who you are as a person.

I am a teacher, and I've discovered that it is my one best thing. Besides the classes I teach at the university, I've always been involved in Sunday school classes, Bible studies, and worship teaching. Teaching fulfills my gifting, and so it is water to my thirsty soul.

Through the years as Genevieve's Alzheimer's disease progressed, we would take her to church, and Sharon would sit with her while I taught the Sunday school lesson. But when our son started middle school, my wife felt the call to be more involved with the youth program and wanted to teach his Sunday school class. I supported her desire to follow her call, and I also thought it would provide a break from the rigors of caregiving. I promised to keep an eye on Genevieve and was sure it would be OK. And it was OK—for a while. But as the months went by, Genevieve became increasingly agitated in my class and couldn't sit through an entire session.

Church was the one thing Genevieve still had in her social life, and we didn't feel it was the right time to lose that connection. I decided, for that season of my life, to give up teaching at the church. Taking Genevieve to church, getting her some coffee, sitting with her in my old class, and helping her negotiate the worship service became my Sunday task.

I really missed teaching, and I was humbled to give up my "up-front" job to take a "behind-the-scenes" job. But I experienced an undeniable joy from faithfully serving someone in need. I would have times to teach in the future, but at that time in my life, there was a "rhythm of rightness" that called me to help Genevieve hang on to church just a bit longer.

In your service of caregiving, you must balance many responsibilities and obligations. How do you know when you are achieving the correct balance? First, you will hear from the people who love you the most. They'll give you feedback on whether you're giving yourself the proper care or nurture, because they can be much more objective about seeing you as you really are. Second, your own body will give you messages, such as whether you always feel tired or get sick often. These are distinct messages that you are out of balance and need to care for yourself. Ultimately, the Spirit of God, who lives in you, will give you assurances about the season of your life. On the outside, the activities or relationships you give up may not make sense to others or even to yourself. But if you know that God has called you to give up something for a time in order to focus on caregiving, you will experience this undeniable "rhythm of rightness."

Morning Prayer

May I Let Things Slip through the Cracks

"Martha, Martha," the Lord answered, "you are worried and upset
about many things, but only one thing is needed. Mary has chosen
what is better, and it will not be taken away from her."

LUKE 10:41–42

I don't know about you, but my schedule as a caregiver is packed
with things to do, and one of those "things" is not "spend some
downtime with my loved one just doing nothing." The list can
seem endless: keeping doctor appointments and physical therapy
sessions, dividing medications and placing in a box, paying bills,
bathing, dressing, shopping, cleaning, changing, cooking, feeding, brushing teeth, putting to bed. And this is a normal day; it
doesn't include special needs that may arise, such as going to the
hospital for treatment or needing to see a specialist. As a caregiver, there always is something else to do, and that "something
else" is usually an important thing that must be done.

Such was the case one day when Genevieve was in the
early stages of Alzheimer's. She went out for a short unsuper-
vised walk, which was her habit at the time and appropriate to
her capabilities. But on this occasion, she got lost. She knocked
on the door of a kind soul, who called the staff at her partial
assistance retirement center. A driver came to pick her up. But
Genevieve was highly agitated, angry, and embarrassed over the
whole ordeal. She began roaming the halls, complaining to the
manager of the building, and then she called our house.

Since Sharon was at work, I went over to calm Genevieve down. But at that particular stage of her disease, she was too distressed to be calmed by words. Finally, out of desperation, I saw a deck of cards on her table. I started to deal the cards, not even knowing which game we would play. We eventually landed on playing solitaire—together! But the diversion had its desired effect as Genevieve began to relax, and we began to have a normal conversation.

Total time? I played cards with Genevieve for about three hours. Thoughts popped into my head constantly about how I didn't have this kind of time to waste on card games:

- I have to complete my writing project.
- I should prepare for class.
- I should call the pharmacy and order medications for the next month.
- I need to sort through some mail.
- I've got some bills I need to pay.

A constant machine-gun volley of these kinds of thoughts kept coming to mind as I forced myself to stay seated, trying to focus on nothing more than red nine on black ten and Genevieve's needs.

The truth is, however, that I was doing the really needed thing. All those things I was so concerned about were important things and did eventually need to be done. But there is always something important that needs to be done. There are times when we must shove those "important" things aside and let them fall through the cracks in order to spend the necessary time caring for, nurturing, listening to, and comforting the one who is in our charge. We are often so busy with caregiving tasks that we don't take the time to *connect* with the ones we care for.

Jesus teaches us this lesson in his encounter with Martha and Mary. Martha was involved in important things that really needed to be done. But Mary was focused on listening to and connecting with Jesus—the really important thing. When Martha protested that Mary wasn't helping her with all the work, Jesus gently said, "Martha, Martha, ... you are worried and upset about many things, but only one thing is needed. Mary has chosen what is better, and it will not be taken away from her" (Luke 10:41–42).

In my job of caregiving, I want to be a person who is willing to let important things slip through the cracks so I can love, nurture, and comfort my loved one. There is always something to be done. May I never let those things prevent me from taking the time to make a true connection with the person to whom I give care.

Evening Reflection

Life, Merry-go-rounds, and Getting It Right

> *"The LORD your God has blessed you in all the work of your hands. He has watched over your journey through this vast desert. These forty years the LORD your God has been with you, and you have not lacked anything."*
>
> DEUTERONOMY 2:7

We tend to think of life as linear—just one occurrence after another until we reach the end of life. But in reality, life is more like a merry-go-round in that we repeat many of the same patterns and practice the same behaviors again and again. Think about the many times you've had arguments with loved ones and found yourself repeating the same lines over and over. Think about the problems in your life. Are they the same ones you were having five or ten years ago? We all like to comfort our-selves in the same ways, use the same patterns and beliefs in solving problems, and rely on the same strengths. Life is not an endless string of unrelated cause-and-effect actions; we are utterly predictable in the manner in which we live.

In our caregiving, we perform in much the same way. When we greet our loved one, we often use the same words. When we deal with the problems and challenges of their illness or limitation, we think in terms of using our same resources and strengths. And, sadly, when we encounter relational difficulties with our loved one, we tend to make the same mistakes over and over. We get on a merry-go-round of behavior that seldom results in solving the issue and often erodes our emotional capacity to cope. For instance, we often get into food fights, insisting they eat something that is good for them while they resist our efforts. We try to force our loved one to take a bath while they insist, "I don't *need* a bath." We say one thing; they say another.

Most of the issues that caregivers and care receivers lock into are totally predictable and recurring. I think of the children of Israel, who were forced to wander in the wilderness for forty years because of their sin. Think about the merry-go-round they were on as they covered the same ground again and again. But God took them on the journey for a specific reason—more than just punishment for their sins. In their wanderings they became familiar with themselves as the people of God, learned to wor-ship and serve God, and began to appreciate his greatness. Even as God was angry with the people for their sin, he blessed them and watched over them.

Did the people become wise? The rest of the story of the people of Israel reveals that they made some of the same fool-ish mistakes from generation to generation. But in the process the hope is that they became a wiser people because of their repetitious patterns.

Many of our frustrations and mistakes in relating to the person we give care for are due to our own patterns. We need to figure out that we *can* do things differently and perhaps achieve a different result. We need to avoid senseless power struggles and ask ourselves, "Is this issue really that important?" We need to change our behaviors and try new things to see if we get different results. And we must always relate our "wandering" to the spiritual dimension that God is with us and wants us to learn to do something new. That "something new" may be practicing a new behavior pattern, developing a new component in our character, or just realizing that we need to be open to God's leading.

As you go through the merry-go-round of caregiving, look to the patterns you keep perpetuating. Try to learn to do something different, and become a wiser caregiver and servant of God.

DAY 26

Morning Prayer

May I Be Open to Transition

> *He is like a tree planted by streams of water,*
> *which yields its fruit in season*
> *and whose leaf does not wither.*
> *Whatever he does prospers.*

PSALM 1:3

Ellen was a dedicated mother and caregiver to her son, Caleb, who had Down syndrome. For years, she and her husband had faithfully raised Caleb, taught him, and worked with him to reach the point of independence. But when the day came for Caleb to move into a halfway house, Ellen wasn't able to let go.

Ellen told me, "Through all these years we've invested to get him to this point, we've developed a closeness and a companionship. I know this is best for him, and I want him to succeed, but I'm just not sure I'm ready to give up the relationship I've had with him all these years. It's hard for me to believe I'll never be his caregiver again, where he's totally dependent on me."

We can simply chalk up Ellen's experience to the transition all mothers go through when they launch their children and experience the empty nest. But I believe to do so would be a mistake. You see, my wife and I experienced the same loss and transition when it came to Genevieve. When her Alzheimer's had progressed to the point where we could no longer care for her, she went to a unit that offered twenty-four-hour-a-day supervision.

One of the first times we went to see Genevieve, her hair looked different, her fingernails were painted, and a thick layer of makeup had been applied on her face. Not only did she have a "look" that was not representative of our care for her, but when we went to her room, she looked at an aide and asked, "Is it OK if I go with them?" Our hearts were crushed.

There is a great privilege in being someone's caregiver. You become close, and he or she comes to depend on every aspect of your care. Perhaps you never asked for or even wanted the job of caregiving in the first place, but now that you've been in the position for so long, you've become accustomed to the connection and process. You have integrated the role of caregiver into your being.

To lose that position isn't an easy thing, but it will surely happen one day. Maybe your loved one will get better or become more independent. Maybe they will transition to a higher level of care than what you can provide, or maybe they will pass away. But when the change comes, you may well be surprised that you don't like being displaced and separated from the job and relationship that have become a part of your nature.

There is a natural season to caregiving. As surely as you have moved into the job, there will come a time when you will give up the privilege. God has planted you, and the caregiving fruit is borne by you only for a time. When it is time for you to let go and transition to a new season, you will feel many different things—joy, relief, gratitude, and peace. But you'll also experience grief and sadness over the reality that you may never again be used in that particular way in your life.

Do not fight to hold on or become angry at the transition, but rather embrace it as a natural part of God's timing. Just as children grow up and leave the home, so too will your caregiving charge become the responsibility of another. May we be willing to embrace the job of caregiving, but may we also be willing to embrace the transition when it is time to let go.

 *Evening Reflection*

Refusing to Facilitate Craziness

If any of you lacks wisdom, he should ask God, who gives generously to all without finding fault, and it will be given to him. But when he asks, he must believe and not doubt, because he who doubts is like a wave of the sea, blown and tossed by the wind. That man should not think he will receive anything from the Lord; he is a double-minded man, unstable in all he does.

JAMES 1:5–8

Larry had a good heart, but he also had unreasonable expectations. Although Larry had been a successful accountant and accomplished musician, Parkinson's disease, diagnosed when he was in his forties, had robbed him of much of his physical skills.

When he and his wife, Marcy, came to see me, it was evident that he had been terrorizing the house for quite some time. When I asked Marcy what she did in her spare time, she told me that Larry didn't like her to leave so she had cut out almost all of her activities. When I asked her about her friends, she told me that Larry needed her most of the time so she didn't have time for friends. When I inquired if any of their friends came to see her, she gave Larry a tentative glance and said, "People just don't come by much anymore." At this, Larry launched into a tirade about how irresponsible and uncaring their friends were and how none of them understand his situation. "Those people at church will never be welcome in my home again," he said in stammering speech, explaining how these "hypocrites" were unresponsive to his needs. Marcy sat and listened, wishing she could fade into the woodwork and disappear.

There are many tough jobs as a caregiver, but one of the toughest is learning what not to do. Larry needed care, but the fact was that Marcy was making many modifications to make sure Larry didn't get angry. He didn't want her to have friends, so in order to keep him pacified, she stopped having friends. He didn't like her being away from him, so she avoided his outbursts by staying at home.

As caregivers, we will often change our behavior—even though it may be uncalled for—in order to facilitate our loved one's moods, likes, dislikes, or dysfunctions. Not only does this not do our care receiver any good; it also tends to make our lives dysfunctional as we facilitate the craziness of our loved one.

Jesus was patient with imperfections, but he never facilitated this type of craziness. Just look at the way he handled the religious leaders of his day. Jesus gave these men every chance to hear the clear message of the gospel. But when they asked him for a miracle on demand, Jesus declared, "A wicked and adulterous generation asks for a miraculous sign! But none will be given it except the sign of the prophet Jonah" (Matthew 12:39). To paraphrase his message, Jesus was saying, "If you want a sign, it is your issue. Face yourself. I will have nothing else to say to you until you are ready to deal with the truth of your own issues."

Jesus was loving and patient, but he never hesitated to confront a person with the truth they needed to face. If Jesus did not facilitate the crazy and unreasonable behavior of people, then we can also confront unjust and unreasonable behavior.

Larry had a good heart, but I confronted him about his anger. He was angry over many things—losing his health, his career, and many of his skills. His anger was understandable. But he was taking his anger out on Marcy, his church, and almost all of his friends.

When Marcy also learned to confront Larry's anger instead of facilitating it, Larry began to express his feelings in a constructive way, which led him eventually to connect instead of isolate. When we learn to confront destructive behavior, we usually help our loved one grow, and we find that we recapture a happier and more productive part of our lives.

Morning Prayer

May I Ask for Miracles Both Big and Small

Dear friends, if our hearts do not condemn us, we have confidence before God and receive from him anything we ask, because we obey his commands and do what pleases him.

1 JOHN 3:21–22

It was the morning of the day before my son's birthday party (he was turning six). We were planning to take him to the arcade with his best buddies. However, we were hundreds of miles away from home, trying desperately to get on a plane in Indianapolis, connecting in St. Louis, to get back to our home. It had been snowing all day, and flights had been temporarily grounded.

Finally, a flight was announced that would be leaving for Kansas City. Even though our flight back home was scheduled to be routed through St. Louis, I reasoned that Kansas City was closer to home than Indianapolis, so we should take the flight. Perhaps we could work something out there or maybe rent a car and drive all night, but I had just about exhausted all hopes of getting my son back home for his party.

About forty-five minutes into the flight, I noticed that my little boy was unusually happy. Grumpily I said, "*You* certainly seem happy."

"I am, Daddy," he said. "I prayed to God that I would get home for my birthday party, and so I don't have to worry anymore."

I remember feeling a dull thud in my stomach. You see, two weeks earlier my son had asked Jesus into his life, and I was frightened about what the disappointment of missing his party would do to his fragile faith after confidently praying such a clear prayer. I wrestled back and forth over what to say to prepare him for the inevitable disappointment of not getting back in time. We had just heard the pilot announce that Kansas City was experiencing a tremendous backlog of stranded travelers. It was almost certain there would be no flights leaving Kansas City and highly unlikely there would be any rental cars left.

I finally mustered the courage to have a heart-to-heart talk with my son to explain that sometimes God does not answer yes to our prayers. As I leaned over and opened my mouth, the airplane nudged forward, signaling a downward descent. "Well, folks, you won't believe this one," the pilot said. "We've been told to land in St. Louis to pick up a few passengers before we move on to Kansas City."

"Could it be?" I thought. We landed in St. Louis twenty minutes before our original connection was scheduled to leave. Within thirty minutes, we were in the air, heading toward home, where we not only arrived on time, but our luggage was waiting for us.

As I crawled into bed that night, I was more than a little amazed but also totally humbled by my son's faith. It was a simple prayer by a six-year-old boy who believed that his party would be on God's priority list. But the amazing and overwhelming part to me was that it *was* on God's priority list. God loved my son so much that he was willing to work a window of opportunity to get us home on time.

Now while I know from my seminary training that prayer, faith, and God's omnipotence are a little more complicated, it was clear that God was honoring the faith of my little boy—a faith I seemed to be too "knowledgeable" to possess in my advanced years, a faith I longed to have once more.

What is keeping us from praying for miracles both big and small? What makes us think God is not interested in that appointment opening up at the doctor's office? Why wouldn't God want the medicine or therapy to go down easier? Why shouldn't God heal the person for whom we are giving care? Don't forget: God is very active in your caregiving, and not all the care depends on *your* ability to provide it.

Will God get me to St. Louis every time so I can make my connection? Maybe not, but I will be a better person for exercising the faith of a little child. May we, this day and every day, have the faith of a child to involve God in our lives and ask him for miracles both big and small.

Evening Reflection

Oh!

Confess your sins to each other and pray for each other so that you may be healed. The prayer of a righteous man is powerful and effective.

JAMES 5:16

"Oh, oh, oh, oh." With every step Genevieve took, she moved in a repetitious machine gun of "oh, oh, oh, oh."

"Are you in pain?" I would ask patiently.

No answer would come, just more "oh, oh, oh, oh."

"Can I get something for you?" I would ask, now a bit perturbed.

Again, only "oh, oh, oh, oh," would come out of her mouth.

I would hold my tongue. I would try to resist my obsession with her noise. I would try to talk myself out of my annoyance.

But in the end, I would explode. "Genevieve, stop saying 'oh' over and over again!"

She would raise her eyebrows, and a look of fear would come over her face as she said louder, "Oh, oh, oh, oh."

What was going on in Genevieve's brain for those several months when all she could say was "oh"? It was probably just one of those things that happened as the brain was assaulted with the damage of disease. But the word haunts me now. I sometimes wonder if it was Genevieve's painful response to having her memory wiped clean like a dry-erase board. Or her response to the painful arthritis that plagued her final years. Or perhaps even her response to the emotional trauma she had borne earlier in her life.

I can try to convince myself otherwise, but somehow I know that Genevieve was in pain as she served up the steady diet of the annoying word. And all I could say to her pain was something that ended with anger and frustration. I saw the pain on her face and promised I wouldn't blow up again, but somehow it got to me and I would get angry. I did many things right as a caregiver, but I did several things that were just plain wrong. It saddens my heart to think I couldn't do better when faced with need and pain.

In our caregiving efforts, all of us will make mistakes and mistreat the persons whom we love and care for. Some of us will not be able to hold our tongues, and so we'll say emotionally damaging things. Some of us will fall into fits of rage where we act out physically. Caregiving can do that to a person—you've had all you can take and there is no relief in sight. Caregivers, no matter the walk of life, are as prone as anyone else to reaching the limits of tolerance and slipping into behavior that is damaging to the person who is receiving care.

What do you do when you know you've slipped into the abyss of being disrespectful, harmful, or abusive? I hope the answer you find is this: "I get on my knees and get help." When confronted by Jesus with their spiritual sin and wayward actions, the Pharisees practiced defensiveness and hostility. But those who were humble—the woman at the well, Zacchaeus the tax collector, the woman caught in adultery, for example—were willing to admit their wrongs and change their ways. Stubbornness and secrecy only allow us to continue our sinful ways.

When you find yourself slipping into inappropriate or just plain wrong behaviors or attitudes, tell people. Tell God, who will forgive you. Tell others, who will give you the relief and encouragement you need to get back on track. None of us are immune from doing wrong, even when we happen to be doing most of the job of caregiving right.

DAY 28

Morning Prayer

May I Listen to the Stories of Other Caregivers

*I long to see you so that I may impart to you some
spiritual gift to make you strong—that is, that you and I
may be mutually encouraged by each other's faith.*

ROMANS 1:11–12

As a backyard astronomer, I love to take my telescope on particularly dark evenings and search the heavens for the faint smudges of light in my eyepiece that are galaxies. They aren't easy to spot with my small instrument, but there are literally millions in the visual field on any given evening. The thought I really love is that the light from the galaxies I spot has actually made a trek of thousands of years to reach my eyes because of the immense distance between those galaxies and the earth. I am actually viewing in the present something thousands of years in the past. It is an elementary lesson in the nature of relativity.

Time and space do funny things to light, and they also do funny things when we think about our pasts and the great legacies. We have a rich history that tells the story of faithfulness, faith, and love. Like light from the distant past, these stories stand as truth and are available to listen to if we will only turn our attention to them. I realize it is no small task to pay attention and listen because the press of caregiving is great, but let me remind you of just a few of the echoes of the past:

David triumphed over the Philistine with a sling and a stone; without a sword in his hand he struck down the Philistine and killed him.

1 SAMUEL 17:50

See the light from the past: There is no task you cannot handle, because the Lord is on your side.

Abram believed the LORD, and he credited it to him as righteousness.

GENESIS 15:6

See the light from the past: God is faithful to honor our faithfulness, even when we don't know where we are going or see any possibility that life will meet our expectations.

Joseph said to them, "Don't be afraid. Am I in the place of God? You intended to harm me, but God intended it for good to accomplish what is now being done, the saving of many lives."

GENESIS 50:19–20

See the light from the past: Despite injustices that may exist, God is active and using the circumstances of life to bring about his will in his perfect timing.

Ruth replied, "Don't urge me to leave you or to turn back from you. Where you go I will go, and where you stay I will stay. Your people will be my people and your God my God."

RUTH 1:16

See the light from the past: Even in the midst of tragedy, God is hopeful and is working toward redemption of our situations and the whole of humanity.

As I devoted myself day in and day out to the task of caregiving, I often thought of the examples of other caregivers:

- my cousin, who has taken on the caregiving job not just once but seven times and who sings the praises of God through it all
- my friend Louisa, who cares not only for her son who has cancer but also for her husband with leukemia and who speaks constantly of God's goodness
- my friends Jonathan and Rebecca, who have twins battling heart ailments that require surgery after surgery and who look to God for his moment-by-moment provision of strength

All around us are people who have faced unbelievably hard situations. From them we can be reminded of God's goodness and faithfulness and be encouraged in our own work of caregiving.

Evening Reflection

A Time to Reflect and Renew

This I call to mind
and therefore I have hope:
Because of the LORD's great love we are
not consumed,
for his compassions never fail.
They are new every morning;
great is your faithfulness.

LAMENTATIONS 3:21–23

One of my counseling clients, Margaret, once described a really awful day she'd had. That morning, the toaster broke and she couldn't have her typical breakfast. As she opened the refrigerator, a gallon of milk fell out, gushing everywhere and splashing on her clothes. She cleaned up the mess, changed her clothes, and rushed out to pick up her father for an appointment with the doctor. When she arrived to pick him up, she discovered he had put his shirt on backwards. He refused to take it off to put it on correctly. When she got to the appointment, she had to fill out three pages of paperwork, but then they waited for two hours before being told they had to go to the hospital for more tests. But as they went to the car, her dad lost his balance and fell, hurting his wrist. After X-raying the wrist, the orthopedic surgeon told her that her dad would need to have a pin inserted into his wrist. Finally, after getting her dad settled, Margaret sat down to dinner—and her son informed her that he was failing algebra.

We've all had days like this—difficult days because of the mood of the one we care for, because of power struggles, because of accidents and messes, or because we received bad news about the prognosis of our loved one. On these days nothing went right, and each step toward getting something accomplished seemed to put us two steps behind.

On days like this, evenings can be the toughest—when we reflect on what happened during the day. It can wear on us terribly. Many times I've faced situations in which I can't imagine how things could work out and everywhere I turn I see more problems. These are the days when I want to pull the sheets over my head and stay in bed. I feel drained of hope.

When we reflect on particularly discouraging days, it robs us of joy and of the hope that God is indeed working on our behalf. The prophet Jeremiah had many such discouraging days. He had the unpleasant task of bringing bad news and overseeing much of the dismantling of the kingdom of Israel. Each day for Jeremiah surely seemed like the low point—how could the news get any worse? He had to have wanted to crawl into bed and refuse to get up the next day. Yet day after day, amidst great discouragement, Jeremiah got up. How did he do it?

> *I remember my affliction and my wandering,*
> *the bitterness and the gall.*
> *I well remember them,*
> *and my soul is downcast within me.*
> *Yet this I call to mind*
> *and therefore I have hope:*
> *Because of the LORD's great love we are*
> *not consumed,*
> *for his compassions never fail.*
> *They are new every morning;*
> *great is your faithfulness.*

LAMENTATIONS 3:19–23

Jeremiah remembered that God would be there in the morning. The hope of God's being on his side, working on his behalf even in discouraging circumstances, turned his reflection to renewal. We will have bad days, and we will slip into discouragement at the end of these days. But we have the renewing hope that God is faithful and that there is a dawn each day. Let us always remember that, as the psalmist declares, "weeping may remain for a night, but rejoicing comes in the morning" (Psalm 30:5).

DAY 29

Morning Prayer

May I Hold to Precious Moments

> *We were gentle among you, like a mother*
> *caring for her little children.*
>
> 1 THESSALONIANS 2:7

I received another dreaded call. It was another bad day in a string of very bad days. Genevieve had reached a brain error where each minute of the day she was convinced someone was coming to take her somewhere. By this time, she was in a supervised care facility where she had done fairly well, but the facility wasn't able to provide one-on-one direction. From the moment Genevieve got up each day, she wanted to go outside and find the person who was going to take her somewhere. She would wander to each car and test the doors to see if they were unlocked. When she found an unlocked door, she would crawl in and wait to go somewhere.

None of us knew how long this behavior would last. It had gone on for about two weeks when we came to the conclusion that we needed to move Genevieve to a facility with the capability of managing this new tendency to wander. It was a painful decision that would move her to the highest level of care for an Alzheimer's patient. It was a decision that came at an inconvenient time because of busy schedules with kids and work. And this decision had to be made quickly, since each new day at her present facility brought new risks and problems.

But as I drove over to calm my mother-in-law, I reflected on what a prize of a woman she was and how precious she had been to me through the years. I remembered how she would hug me and greet me—just to make me feel welcome. I remembered how she would cut out newspaper clippings she thought I'd be interested in reading and how she cultivated her love of football and baseball because she knew I liked those sports. I remembered her suppers, which included favorites of everyone at the table to enjoy. I remembered her selfless giving of money so people could have nicer things than she had had, her funny ideas about politics and how the human body worked, and the way she would find just the right present to make Christmas special. She was a special woman who gave us so many precious moments to cherish.

When I got to the care facility, we sat together while I made the necessary phone calls to prepare for her move. I gazed into her blank eyes. I caressed the back of her hand and stroked her hair. I reassured her that I would be there for her.

Of course, there was no response from her. She did not verbally acknowledge a single thing I said; she didn't respond to any of my physical touch. Had you been observing us, you might have concluded that we made no connection that day. But in actuality, it was one of the most precious times I had with Genevieve during her last days of Alzheimer's. You see, all those lovely and wonderful things about this woman were still in there somewhere, even though she could not locate them in her memory. But all of who she was—her strength, humor, care, loyalty, and giving nature—were still in there. Through my memory and my holding on to what was so great about her, we were able to share once again the gentle, connecting, person-to-person intimacy we sometimes take for granted when both parties are in good health.

You will experience times when problems or needs seem to overwhelm the fact that you are caring for a precious person with a precious character full of precious moments. He or she may not even be able to access that preciousness anymore. But you can hold on to those things that are the greatest and best through your memories and interactions. May we always strive to hold on to precious moments and the people with whom we are connected.

Evening Reflection

All She Wants Is to Go Home

Just as man is destined to die once, and after that to face judgment, so Christ was sacrificed once to take away the sins of many people; and he will appear a second time, not to bear sin, but to bring salvation to those who are waiting for him.

HEBREWS 9:27–28

Death can be difficult to watch. When we remove all the platitudes, such as "death is just a part of life," the actual process of the soul's letting go of the body is often tortured and exhausting. I have been present at many deaths, and while the actual moment of death can be peaceful and resolved, the days and weeks leading up to the departure are usually hard. The body is built to live, and so it struggles to hang on, even when the dying person would rather give up the fight.

Hallie was such a woman. Hallie had fought and survived cancer for almost twelve years. During that time, she had finished raising her children and getting them through college, seen two grandchildren born, and traveled to experience the great art of Europe. But the last three months were particularly hard, and it was clear that the cancer was going to have its way.

Hallie's daughter, who had been a wonderful caregiver for her mother during many illnesses, pleaded with her mother, "You have licked this before, and you can hang in there again." Hallie whispered something through the tubing in her mouth that only her daughter could understand. Hallie's daughter kissed her on the cheek and said, "OK, Momma. OK." She turned to the rest of us and said, "All she wants is to go home." Hallie was dead an hour later.

In our culture, we're trained to fight death and deny that it looms for all of us. We don't get a pass because of our belief in Jesus. All of humanity is destined to die and face judgment. We have a hard time facing this because of our natural tendency toward denial, but we certainly have difficulty with death as caregivers. Our natural tendency is to hold on, stave off, and fight for just another day. But as any caregiver will tell you, there is a time that is appointed for a person's death. You may offer the best care in the world and the brightest and best medical minds may be working on the case, but when it's time to die, people will die.

The cold reality isn't meant to make us hard; it's meant to make us connected. Death makes us as caregivers realize there is a time to let go of our charge and place them into the arms of God. It is the ultimate truth that caregiving teaches that life is not in our control. When we come to peace with the fact that there will be a time to let go, we can focus our energies on connecting with the person to whom we have given care. We can focus on his or her enduring qualities that we'll remember after death; we can focus on speaking words of affection and good-byes. Nothing is sadder or more disturbing than to see a caregiver hold on to his or her loved one, insisting that doctors take extraordinary and desperate measures to salvage life and passionately demanding that others not give up hope of a recovery. Even though we've been connected to our loved one, we cannot go on the journey with him or her after death. As caregivers, we must emulate Hallie's daughter and release them and let go.

The good news, of course, is that if our loved ones know the Lord, death does *not* have the final word. They are covered and welcomed by the living God. We cannot save our loved ones from being stung by death, but we can hang on to the good news that the sting of death will not gain the ultimate victory. With the apostle Paul, we declare, "Death has been swallowed up in victory. Where, O death, is your victory? Where, O death, is your sting?" (1 Corinthians 15:54–55).

DAY 30

Morning Prayer

May I Truly Learn to Honor

No matter how many promises God has made, they are "Yes" in Christ. And so through him the "Amen" is spoken by us to the glory of God. Now it is God who makes both us and you stand firm in Christ. He anointed us, set his seal of ownership on us, and put his Spirit in our hearts as a deposit, guaranteeing what is to come.

2 CORINTHIANS 1:20–22

Caregivers are typically a humble lot. They tend to have the gifts of service and of mercy as they function as the support beneath someone. They tend to do their work in the background and never seem to be in the spotlight. There's nothing wrong with this humility, but too often I hear caregivers talk about themselves disrespectfully as being unworthy or unimportant. I can't tell you the number of times I've asked caregivers to tell me about themselves and received the answer, "There's nothing special about me."

If we are to honor God, we must believe we are honorable and worthy of respect. In spite of our sins, God has taken an interest in us. He bought us at a price, making us his prized possession in whom he is pleased (see 1 Corinthians 7:23).

God could have created anything to give him honor or praise. But he chose to create human beings such as you and me—humans made in his image with an eternal soul; humans who have a choice on whether to live for and glorify him, humans he appoints to be colaborers in bringing about his purpose in creation. Out of all created things, we are built by God to have a special relationship like none other.

How do we get to the point where we really honor ourselves as created beings made in God's image? We soak in the fact the same way that a piece of wood gets waterlogged after staying in the water for a long time.

When I married my wife, Sharon, I would have sworn to you that I loved her as much as I could. But now, after many years of marriage, I see how much more I've grown in the truth of my love. Did I not love her when we first married? Of course I did, but my capacity to realize the depths of my love has grown. So too we may realize that God loves us and honors us now, but we need to go back over the truth again and again. Truth needs time to penetrate.

God is serious about his "yes" to us. He has anointed the very essence of who we are; he owns us, and he put his Spirit in us. He would not do these things if we were not honored colaborers with him. As caregivers, it is up to us to appropriate the honor he has bestowed on us and translate it into the sense of regarding ourselves as honorable. In this way we acknowledge him as the truly honorable and special God he is.

I often repeat the following to remind myself of the powerful "yes" God has given me: Yes. God, you said yes. Yes, I was favored and highly prized. Yes, I was worthy, and you were more than willing to walk with me. Yes, I was hurt and was able to be healed as you hemmed my heart. Yes, I bowed my head, and at once your hand held my head and lifted my eyes to caress my crown and commission my conscience. Yes, I teetered on the edge, and you took me and tutored me by your loving, teaching touch. Yes, I am a part. Yes, I am unique. Yes, I am a slave. Yes, I am served. Yes, I am perfected. Yes, I am last. Yes, I am first.

Yes, I am wanting. Yes, I am fulfilled. Yes, I am broken. Yes, I am whole. Yes, yes, yes. I am one loved, one held, one worthy. Yes, God, you said yes.

Today I want to learn how to honor God. Today I want to learn how to regard myself as honorable. May we seek the truth about who we are and commit ourselves to honoring God.

Evening Reflection
Learning Self-Sacrifice

May God himself, the God of peace, sanctify you through and through. May your whole spirit, soul and body be kept blameless at the coming of our Lord Jesus Christ. The one who calls you is faithful and he will do it.

1 THESSALONIANS 5:23–24

When it comes to caregiving, I ask two questions consistently: Why caregiving? And why now? Or to put it another way, What is it about caregiving that compels God to be so bent on using this experience in the lives of believers? And why is caregiving becoming so prevalent at this time in human history? Although I certainly don't have all the answers, I have a clue about at least a partial response.

First, caregiving is the closest thing we experience to true, self-sacrificing love. Many people think of God's love in terms of "unconditional." It *is* unconditional, but more than that, it is self-sacrificing. Self-sacrifice means we have one plate of food, and you and I both need it to survive. If we split it, neither of us will survive. I look at you and say, "Take and eat." This is the kind of love that God has for us. To paraphrase Romans 5:8, while we were in the most desperate of conditions and needed God's compassion or care, Jesus placed himself in need of the same and gave himself for us. There is no way for us to pay Jesus back for his sacrifice on our behalf. All we can do is accept the benefit of the grace he gives.

Caregiving gives us such an opportunity to learn to be self-sacrificing. We all have things to do in our lives besides giving care to someone in need. But the fact that we give care to someone who cannot care for us teaches us about the purity and sacrifice of God's love and in turn makes us more giving. The reality is that many of those we care for will not get better and will languish or even die. To care for someone who cannot give back is a glimpse of what it is like to share grace. Caregiving teaches us about true, self-sacrificing, godly love.

But why now? Why is caregiving much more prevalent in our world? Medical science has made it possible for the average life span to reach almost eighty, and most will live far into their eighties. People have always cared for their elderly loved ones, but never have there been so many for whom to care. What's more, medical science has made it possible to live with conditions that would have been terminal even fifteen years ago. In other words, a condition that would have killed a premature child a few years ago can now be treated as a chronic illness. As a result, more people in chronically ill conditions can be kept alive.

These are a few reasons more people are in need of care, but why did God choose *now*? We've just left the twentieth century, where my generation was referred to as the "me" generation—a generation regarded as selfish, self-absorbed, and unconcerned about others. As part of that generation, I confess that the mind-set has often been to escape responsibility and leave it to "the other guy" to take care of others. But at this very time in history,

God has enabled our sick, elderly, and infirm loved ones to live longer than at any other time in history. Perhaps my generation could ignore the other guy's need, but it is impossible to ignore the needs of our children, spouses, and parents. In short, I believe God chose *now* in order to mold this generation into a *giving* generation. Caregiving is the anvil through which God is hammering out his love into our characters.

Why caregiving, and why now? Because God wants us to learn self-sacrificing love, and he is particularly interested in transforming a generation of self-focused people. To love and to overcome our selfish desires and ambitions—this is always the transforming work of God in the redemption and sanctification of his people. May we, by his grace, be willing followers in the process of becoming more like Christ.